MW01519232

FOR THOSE WHO BELIEVE

Renewal of the Church Through the Ministry of the Holy Spirit

Dr. Gwendolyn Long Cudjoe

PRESS

For Those Who Believe
by Dr. Gwendolyn Long Cudjoe

Printed in the United States of America

ISBN 1-594676-92-5

www.xulonpress.com

DEDICATION

To My Mother

I dedicate this book to the loving memory of my mother, Mrs. Frances Louise Long. Thank you, Mother, for loving me unconditionally, rejoicing with me in times of happiness, standing with me, teaching me to have courage in times of trials, never asking anything of me, but always giving me all of you and all that was yours. You sacrificed much in order for me to strive higher and turn my dreams into reality. Thank you, Mother, for modeling true motherhood for me, so that I would know how to love my children as you have loved me. Thank you, God, that my mother is now seated in heavenly places with Christ Jesus. I love you, Mother.

To My Children

I dedicate this book to my precious first-born, Frances Louise Cudjoe Waters, and my devoted son-in-law, James Lucian Waters (whom I love like a son), and to my angel baby, Gabriella Elizabeth Cudjoe.

Your love and your prayers have sustained me through the writing of this book. You are God's perfect gifts to me, and you make my life worth living. I love you unconditionally as my mother loved me. Stay close to Jesus and nothing shall be impossible for you.

To My Grandchildren

I dedicate this book to William James Cudjoe Waters (age 3) and Joshua Brouk Cudjoe Waters (age 2). Nana loves you.

ACKNOWLEDGEMENTS

God has graciously sent into my life spirit-filled Christians who taught me how to walk with Jesus as I began my spiritual journey in Cambridge, Massachusetts. Rev. Dr. LeRoy Attles, my father in the ministry taught me to serve God in season and out of season. Queen Mother Frances J. Pierce, my spiritual mother, taught me how to stand in the midst of the storms and believe God for the victory. Rev. Albertha Merriman, my spiritual mentor, my prayer warrior, taught me how to minister to God's people and how to remain faithful without seeking recognition for self. Rev. Florence Petersen and Rev. Jay and Ingrid Broadnax, my friends, have been strong spiritual support for me as I traveled the perilous highway of life. I love you. Thank you.

When I moved to Houston, Texas, God sent other spiritually mature Christians to lead and walk with me on the next phase of my journey. Bishop John R. Bryant and Rev. Dr. Cecelia Williams Bryant have been a great source of spiritual strength for me. They refused to allow the devil to steal, kill and destroy the vision that God had placed in my spirit. They opened many doors for me to serve the African Methodist Episcopal Church, and I shall always be grateful. Mrs. Mary Helen Reed, my spiritual mother in Houston, has under girded me with prayer. Rev. M.C. Cooper and the Wayman Chapel A.M.E. Church family participated in the case study reported in this book. I love you. Thank you.

When I moved to Dallas, Texas, Bishop Bryant and Rev. Dr. Bryant continued to lead me spiritually. And at Paul Quinn College I met other persons who blessed my life. Among them are Ms. Michelle Henry, an angel who painstakingly edited the first draft of this manuscript, President Dwight Fennell, Mrs. Ann Mathews, Dr. Weldon Walton and Dr. Stephen Jones. Also, I must acknowledge my students who studied from an unpublished draft of this manuscript and offered their suggestions: Pamela Fields, Yori Garrick, Trudy Ann Gordon, Katrina Trotman, Marco Barker and Marvin Jewell Avant. Beyond Paul Quinn, God smiled on me again and sent another angel, Ms. Cheryl Rhodes, who helped type this manuscript. I love you. Thank you.

Finally, Evangelist Doris Aneise Long, my sister and my best friend. Thank you for the wonderful work on the charts and for permitting me to read the entire book to you. I love you. Thank you.

CONTENTS

ix

LIST OF CHARTS

Preface

Are we as Christians living to please God or to assimilate into the culture in which we live at the expense of the Gospel? How do we respond to the commands of God's word to live holy, when society pressures us to be "tolerant," "politically correct" and "socially correct?" How do we respond to racism, hatred, ordination of homosexuals, same-sex marriage, sexual immorality in the leadership in the church, and other sins?

We must not allow the world to impose upon us an ungodly vision of the world's "tolerance" that produces viewpoints and values that do not align with Holy Scripture. It is time for the church to take a stand for righteousness. Moreover, I believe that as Christians are baptized in the Holy Spirit and serve in the area of their spiritual gifts, we will see a reversal in the pattern of stagnation and decline that has manifested itself in many mainline denominations. We need not invent a new paradigm; we simply must return to God's original paradigm (before the fall of humanity) and refuse to be intimidated by those who want to distort the Gospel of Jesus Christ and live according to the flesh. I believe we can return to God's original plan for us if we seek His face daily and submit to His Lordship in our lives. We need a clearer understanding of how the baptism in the Holy Spirit will enable us to walk as victors every-day and how our spiritual gifts will bring joy in our service to the Body of Christ.

In this book, I will recount the findings of the study I conducted for my doctoral project. This book focuses on two essential ingredients for renewal of the church: believers' baptism in the Holy Spirit and their understanding and utilization of their spiritual gifts. The material presented here is not intended to be exhaustive; however, it offers a means to help us reconsider our position and purpose in the world as Christians, and it outlines recommendations for continual spiritual growth in individuals, families, students in higher education, small groups and con-gregations.

This book is divided into seven chapters. Chapter one, *The Enco*unter, details my personal conversion experience and my quest to advance a commitment to holiness in the church. Chapter two, *The Distractions*, underscores the role of the church and the schemes of Satan to weaken and destroy the core values of Christians. Chapter three, *The Conviction*, delineates the biblical and theological rationale underlying the thesis of this book and surveys the ministry of the Holy Spirit in the Old Testament and the New Testament. Chapter four, *The Renewal of the Church,* provides a historical basis for the study and brief account of selected church movements from 1517 to 2001. Chapter five, *The Case Study*, is an overview of the teaching series, together with demographics of the participants, an outline of their goals, and a synopsis of their understanding of the baptism in the Holy Spirit and spiritual gifts. Chapter six, *The Analysis*, measures and evaluates the effectiveness of the project. Various post-test data were compiled and analyzed to quantify these variables and related outcomes. Chapter seven, *The Power of Prayer*, emphasizes the importance of prayer in living by the power of the Holy Spirit and using spiritual gifts and summarizes the project. The appendices include instruments that were used in the study: (1) pre-test questionnaire, (2) course syllabus, (3) post-test questionnaire, and (4) course evaluation form.

I pray that the Holy Spirit will speak to your heart as you read this book and that the Lord our God will fill you daily with His power for your witness and ministry.

Rev. Dr. Gwendolyn Long Cudjoe
Cedar Hill, Texas 75104
Resurrection Sunday
April 11, 2004

CHAPTER 1

THE ENCOUNTER

*"I love the Lord, for he heard my voice;
he heard my cry for mercy."
(Ps. 116:1)*

For years I vacillated between holy living and secular living. When I attended church services, I knew that following Jesus was my destiny, and I felt convicted for giving Him less than my total commitment. I vowed again and again to surrender my whole life to Jesus, but once I left the safety of the church service and went out with friends, I was lured into sin. This battle raged within me for several years. In my heart, I wanted to live holy for God, but in my flesh, I lacked the power to do so. Willpower alone was no match for the smooth, cunning, and deceptive ways of Satan. I wondered, "Do any other Christians struggle like this? Am I the only one? What is wrong with me?" I echoed the words of Paul,

So I find this law at work: When I want to do good, evil is right there with me. For in my inner being I delight in God's law; but I see another law at work in the members of my body, waging war against the law of my mind and making me a prisoner of the law of sin at work within my members. What a wretched man I am! (Rom. 7:21-24).

I had become so accustomed to my lifestyle that it was difficult to give up the momentary pleasures of sin, while awaiting an eternal reward. There was tension between my desire for immediate gratification and my yearning for future blessings. Would I continually succumb to the temptation to fulfill the present desire of the flesh and forfeit the eschatological promises of the Word of God? I cried out to God and asked God to forgive me over and over again. I finally realized that if I was serious about my walk with God, I had to be open and honest with God. I began to pray on a deeper level and asked God to take away my desire for things and my association with people who were not pleasing to Him. I was miserable, and I felt like a hypocrite.

I could have lingered in this abyss forever, but in November 1983, God graciously sent Bishop Corletta Harris-Vaughn (who was at that time Evangelist Corletta Harris) to my home church, St. Paul African Methodist Episcopal (A.M.E.) Church in Cambridge, Massachusetts, to preach a one-week revival. Although the St. Paul congregation had heard many wonderful sermons over the years, there was something different about Bishop Harris-Vaughn's preaching. She preached and taught us about the baptism in the Holy Spirit and the gifts of the Holy Spirit. The Holy Spirit confirmed in our hearts that this woman was truly from God. For like the Apostle Paul, she could have affirmed, "When I came to you, brothers, I did not come with eloquence or superior wisdom as I proclaimed to you the testimony about God. For I resolved to know nothing while I was with you except Jesus Christ and him crucified. . . My message and my preaching were not with wise and persuasive words, but with a demonstration of the Spirit's power, so that your faith might not rest on men's wisdom, but on God's power" (1 Cor. 2:1-2, 4). Bishop Harris-Vaughn began each service with extended praise and worship. She praised God and condemned sin. She boldly preached the pure, unadulterated, uncompromised Word of God, and signs and wonders accompanied the Word. When the invitation to Christian discipleship was extended at the end of each service, the altar was flooded with people giving their lives to Jesus. Every night as Bishop Harris-Vaughn extended the invitation, she sang, and encouraged people to come to the altar; she never rushed this part of the service, and she always gave assurance that there was room for everyone at the altar, which symbolized the cross of Jesus Christ. Bishop Harris-Vaughn asked three questions as she walked among the people - "Are you saved? Are you sure? If Jesus came back tonight, would He take you to spend eternity with Him?" Those three questions rang in my heart and my mind like resounding cymbals. They reverberated louder and louder every time she repeated the questions.

I had known God since I was a child and was baptized when I was five years old. In my adult years, however, I had strayed away from the church. When my family moved to Massachusetts in 1978, we joined St. Paul by profession of faith, but I still could not answer, "yes" to those three questions, because in my heart I was not sure. My life was not a reflection of my public declaration. I believed in Jesus, but my lifestyle had not changed over the years. I went to church every Sunday, but there was no correlation between the Sunday service and my life during the week. I was not growing spiritually. I had not been urgently challenged to leave my life of sin and live holy. I thought that going to church on Sunday and paying my tithes was all that God required of me. How wrong I was. Bishop Harris-Vaughn's questions pierced my heart and the hearts of others, too, because as she sang and extended the invitation, people rushed to the altar from the main floor of the sanctuary and from the balcony. The altar was flooded with people giving their lives to Jesus. I saw people who frequented clubs and other worldly venues rush to the altar. As I looked at their faces, I could see their sincerity. The Holy Spirit was moving in their spirit and in mine. As I sat in the pew, I had a supernatural encounter with Jesus. I felt that all of my questions were answered in that moment. All the confusion and doubt I had felt for so many years dissipated as the authority of the Word of

God permeated my very soul. I could not contain my new liberation. I got up and rushed to the altar to join the other men, women, boys and girls who had been set free by the Gospel of Jesus Christ. We did not care who saw us. Many of us were crying, men and women alike. We were willing to be broken in the presence of God and the congregation, because we knew that the struggle was finally over. The bondage to sin was broken! True deliverance had come to us. As Bishop Harris-Vaughn led us in the prayer of salvation, we asked God to forgive us for our sins and personalized Romans 10:9 as we repeated the prayer of salvation after her:

> Dear God, please forgive me for my sins. I confess with my mouth that Jesus is Lord, and I believe in my heart that God raised Him from the dead. I accept Jesus Christ as my personal Lord and Savior, and now I am saved.

After each person at the altar uttered the prayer of salvation, Bishop Harris-Vaughn prayed for us, the new converts, to be baptized in the Holy Spirit. Many persons began speaking in tongues immediately. Some received the baptism in the Holy Spirit without even a touch from the Bishop. The rest of us continued to pray. She told us to pray for the baptism in the Holy Spirit, to yearn for it, and to expect God to bestow this blessing upon God's people. She said we could receive the baptism in the Holy Spirit at church, at home, or wherever we were seeking God, and we could be assured that God would answer our prayers.

After the altar call, Bishop Harris-Vaughn ministered throughout the congregation using her spiritual gifts to deliver, strengthen, convict, rebuke, correct, and encourage the people of God. The services began at 7:00 p.m. nightly, and some nights our revival preacher continued ministering until 12:30 a.m. She had an insatiable urgency to proclaim Christ in as many ways as the Holy Spirit enabled her. She said the Holy Spirit had empowered her with all nine of the gifts listed in First Corinthians 12 (which are discussed in greater length later in this book), and through the Holy Spirit we witnessed the gifts in action. Her message was so powerful that people listened and believed. Bishop Harris-Vaughn's ministry reminded me of Philip's ministry in Samaria, of which it is written:

> *Philip went down to a city in Samaria and proclaimed the Christ there. When the crowds heard Philip and saw the miraculous signs he did, they all paid close attention to what he said. With shrieks, evil spirits came out of many, and many paralytics and cripples were healed. So there was great joy in that city* (Acts 8:5-8).

God used Bishop Harris-Vaughn to heal broken hearts, cast out evil spirits, and heal people of cancer, heart disease and a host of other diseases. Rev. Dr. LeRoy Attles, the senior pastor of St. Paul, had worn glasses constantly, but in the revival he was healed. He removed his glasses, hung them up in his secretary's office, and has never put them on again. (That was 21 years ago). Many persons came back with a doctor's written report that they had been healed, including one woman who was healed of breast cancer in the revival service. During the service, Bishop Harris-Vaughn told the woman to go to the restroom and search for the lump. She came back and said she could not find it. Her doctor confirmed in writing that the cancer had disappeared! The revival was so powerful that it lasted for three weeks, instead of one week. People came to Cambridge, Massachusetts, from across the greater Boston area to hear this mighty woman of God and to see God confirm His Word with signs and wonders. Pastor Attles was also baptized in the Spirit, and God gave him the gift of healing. He is still active in the ministry of healing at St. Paul, and he travels around the country preaching and sharing this gift with those who come to hear his powerful word.

St. Paul was renewed and the city experienced an awakening as the woman of God had the faith, courage, and boldness to trust God and to preach and teach on the baptism in the Holy Spirit and the use of spiritual gifts. Bishop Harris-Vaughn preached every night and taught a noonday Bible study each day on the baptism in the Holy Spirit and spiritual gifts. This was St. Paul's first exposure to teaching on the gifts. I attended every Bible study. The church was within walking distance of my job, and my supervisor gave me permission to attend the Bible study on my lunch hour with the understanding that I would work an extra fifteen minutes each day. Words cannot explain how my life was transformed through the preaching and teaching ministry of this committed servant of the Lord Jesus Christ. It was in these meetings that I determined for certain that I would never go back to the ways of the world. I felt fulfilled and happy. I knew I had been delivered from my life of sin and had finally come home to Jesus. I understood Paul's words even more when he said, *"...Who will rescue me from this body of death? Thanks be to God – through Jesus Christ our Lord!" (Rom. 7:24-25).* That was my experience. I could not defeat the enemy alone, and I did not have to because Jesus Christ, my personal Lord and Savior, had already defeated him. Jesus rescued me from a life of sin and offered me a new beginning in Him through the power of the Holy Spirit. In this new beginning, Jesus promised not to bring up my past or make me feel guilty or ashamed. And if you have accepted Jesus Christ as your personal Lord and Savior, you too have been forgiven and there should be no guilt or shame about your past. God said,

> *As far as the east is from the west, so far has he removed our transgressions from us. As a father has compassion on his children so the Lord has compassion on those who fear him (Ps. 103:12-13).*

After I surrendered my heart, mind, body and spirit to the Lord, I found an oasis of tranquility. Even my everyday life challenges were met with the assurance that nothing was too difficult for my God. I learned how to pray and trust Jesus to intervene in my circumstances and lead me to His ark of safety, protection and serenity. Even though the world is filled with uncertainty, I was certain that Jesus would never leave me or forsake me or anyone else who trusts in Him.

I prayed continually for the baptism in the Holy Spirit to empower me so that I could live this Christian life triumphantly. I yearned to lead and teach my thirteen-year-old daughter, Frances (who received the baptism in the Holy Spirit in the first week of the revival), how to live for God and grow spiritually. I did not receive the baptism that night at the altar, but I knew by faith that I would at God's appointed time. Every morning I had my personal devotions in my home at 6:00 a.m., and every morning I prayed for the baptism. Bishop Harris-Vaughn preached a sermon during the revival entitled "Take Back Your Blessings," and that sermon resonated in my spirit. I believed that the enemy had robbed me of my spiritual heritage for a long time, and now it was time for me to take back my blessings. As I made my way to my little altar in my home every morning, I sang praises to God, read the Word of God and prayed for the baptism in the Holy Spirit. This pattern continued for some time, but one morning God answered my prayer in my living room. God baptized me in the Holy Spirit and gave me a prayer language (i.e., speaking in tongues). I was ecstatic! I invited the Holy Spirit to be my comforter and my guide through the wilderness of life and to sustain me as I basked in the wealth of the Holy Spirit's love. I thanked God for this great gift. God gave me a boldness to live for

Him and the power to teach Frances more in-depth about the Gospel of Jesus Christ. And from that point on, we never looked back. We have been in love with Jesus from that day to the present, and we will be in love with Jesus forever.

I am proud to be a part of the Body of Christ. I have a place to belong and an extended family of millions of Christians around the world that I can call sisters and brothers. The true Christian family extends beyond racial, national, denominational, class or cultural lines, because we are all one in Christ Jesus. You ask, "How can that be?" In the natural it sounds impossible, but in the spirit God said, *"You are all sons of God through faith in Christ Jesus, for all of you who were baptized into Christ have clothed yourselves with Christ. There is neither Jew nor Greek, slave nor free, male nor female, for you are all one in Christ Jesus" (Gal. 3:26-28).* I was radiant as I lived each day with my chaste faith that was manifested in every area of my life. I hungered for more of the Word of God. I wished that I could speed-read because my eyes failed to keep up with the pace my spirit had set for my daily reading of God's holy Word. I looked forward to corporate worship and longed for more and more opportunities to praise and glorify God.

In 1986, God called me to preach and teach His holy Word and to lead His people out of darkness into His marvelous light. In the fall of 1986, I entered Gordon-Conwell Theological Seminary in South Hamilton, Massachusetts, to prepare for my life's work.

The Need for Holiness in the Church

After some time, I decided to become more active in my church. I joined ministries in the local church and began attending church meetings. To my dismay, I found a dichotomy between the testimonies expressed in corporate worship experiences and the views expressed in meetings and other church activities. In the corporate worship services, the people praised God and confessed their belief in God's promises and their commitment to live by His commands. However, in other settings (church meetings, the workplace, non-ecclesial) views and actions were expressed that were contrary to the Word of God. As I traveled to other churches and attended seminary, I saw first hand that racism was still alive and doing quite well in Christian circles. I saw Christians endorse worldly doctrines and beliefs that did not comply with the Word of God. Many of those beliefs were translated into lifestyles that made the church look and sound very much like the secular world from which I had fled. I was mortified! I thought about how I had struggled for years to give myself totally to Christ and the church, only to find that too many persons in leadership positions in the church, and those called to lead God's people, were serving two masters. Now that I was saved, had I become self-righteous? Certainly not. The church must always be open to receive anyone who is seeking salvation and to help people overcome their struggles just as I had been helped. However, the church should place those in leadership who have made a commitment to follow Jesus Christ and live by the Word of

God both in church and in the world. It is incumbent upon the leadership to set an example for Christian living. If the leadership compromises the Word of God, the people will, too. But if the leadership stands boldly and courageously on the teachings of the Gospel of Jesus Christ, the people will, too. I had been in the church for a long time, attended service every Sunday, and was never urgently challenged to leave my life of sin. Sin may have been alluded to from time to time, but there were more sermons on the love of God than the judgment of God. This was not peculiar to my local church; the ethos across America was to preach in a way that would not offend the people. It took a spirit-filled woman to come to town and preach the pure, unadulterated Gospel to bring hundreds of people to saving faith. Now that we have accepted this Gospel, we no longer live by secular standards. The encounter with Jesus is greater than anything the world has to offer.

Summary

I am convinced that as the Body of Christ makes a firm commitment to live by biblical principles, we will witness renewal in the church and in society. Church attendance will increase and many lives will be saved from destruction and hell. I know how I struggled until I finally surrendered my life to Jesus Christ by the power of the Holy Spirit. And now I know what I missed out on all the years that I succumbed to the ways of the world instead of following Jesus. I regret that I waited so long to come to

Jesus and allow Him to lead me.

The church universal is facing a spiritual crisis because we are not committed to following Jesus. Jesus calls the church to lead the world, not the world to lead the church. Let us not abdicate our responsibility to advance the Kingdom of God and witness to the world with our lives. Jesus has paid redemption's price so that we can experience abundant life in the here and now and spend eternity with Him, but the gift is only <u>for those who believe</u>.

PRAYER

(SINCERE)

> Holy Father,
>
> Thank You for Jesus Christ, our high priest, who paid redemption's cost for us and opened the door for us to draw near to You with a sincere heart, in full assurance of faith. Thank You, Holy Father, that our hearts are sprinkled with the blood of Jesus to cleanse us from a guilty conscience, and our bodies are washed with the pure water of the Holy Spirit. In Jesus' name. Amen. (Heb. 10:22)

The next chapter will underscore the importance of walking with Jesus daily and the need to actively resist distractions that come to plague us and steal our joy.

CHAPTER 2

THE DISTRACTIONS

*"I am astonished that you are so quickly
deserting the one who called you. . ."*
(Gal. 1:6)

Throughout salvation's history the church has been seen as the cornerstone of love, faith, truth, holiness, unity, and safety. Perhaps the greatest and most sacred moment on earth occurs when believers come together in the corporate worship experience to give reverence, adoration, praise and thanksgiving to God for His loving kindness and mercy toward us, and to receive a revelation from God through the preached word.

Theologically, there is only one church of which Jesus Christ is the head. Unlike a corporation, it cannot merge or consolidate with any other entity. It stands alone and supreme, paid in full by the atonement of Jesus Christ. The members of the church are persons who have accepted Jesus Christ as their Lord and Savior and have made a commitment to live holy. When the Body of Christ lives in unity and holiness, it becomes a living witness to the saving grace of Jesus and experiences the power of the Holy Spirit. Paul wanted this truth to be known to the Ephesians, and his prayer resounds clearly for us today,

> *I pray that according to the riches of His glory, He may grant that you may be strengthened in your inner being with power through His Spirit, and that Christ may dwell in your hearts through faith, as you are being rooted and grounded in love. I pray that you may have the power to comprehend, with all the saints, what is the breadth and length and height and depth, and to know the love of Christ that surpasses knowledge, so that you may be filled with all the fullness of God (Eph. 3:16-19 NRSV).*

God's will is for the church to be united in love and holiness and to impact the world with the good news of the Gospel of Jesus Christ, making disciples of all people.

Regrettably, the Body of Christ is not functioning in unity, love or holiness. Consequently, we are not walking in the full power of the Holy Spirit. Some denominations have endorsed doctrines that are inharmonious with the Word of God. They have compromised the Word of God and drifted away from sound biblical principles in order to be accepted in inter-faith organizations or to fulfill their desire to be viewed as "tolerant." Personal apostasy and denominational apostasy are widespread today. What has happened to the church? Does the church still believe in the holiness of God? Why have we permitted ourselves to be distracted by the crafty, cunning ways of the evil one? Is the church seeking the favor of humanity over the favor of God? Whose side is the church on? Paul warned the Galatians of falling away from the faith and listening to those whose mission was to dilute the Gospel of Jesus Christ: *"I am astonished that you are so quickly deserting the one who called you by the grace of Christ and are turning to a different gospel – which is really no gospel at all" (Gal. 1:6-7)*. Two thousand years later we see that we, like the Galatians, need to be reminded of the truth of God's holy Word. And so I ask, "Is the Bible accurate, and is it sufficiently current and relevant to guide and support believers in the era in which we live? Is the Bible only a book of eschatology? Should we spend our whole life preparing for the hereafter without experiencing victory over sin in this present age?" Don't misunderstand me: I want to go to Heaven and live for eternity with our Lord, but I also want to know that God has made provisions for His people who are left here for an unspecified period of time to occupy until He returns.

As the years have passed, I have become more convinced than ever that the Bible is the one and only book on which we can depend. Its truths are timeless. It transcends time and space. The problem is not with the Word of God. It is with the people of God. It takes faith, courage and the empowerment of the Holy Spirit to live according to biblical principles. God is waiting to fill us with His Spirit, but we have to make a choice between God's ways and secular ways. We cannot expect the world to pat us on the shoulder and encourage us on the journey when we stand for righteousness. That's why it is so good to know that as Christians we are not looking for the applause of women and men. We can rely on the applause of God's angels, who rejoice and shout "Hallelujah" when we make conscious decisions to live for God. Don't be alarmed by persecution. Jesus said,

> *Blessed are those who are persecuted because of righteousness, for theirs is the kingdom of heaven. Blessed are you when people insult you, persecute you and falsely say all kinds of evil against you because of me. Rejoice and be glad, because great is your reward in heaven, for in the same way they persecuted the prophets who were before you (Matt. 5:10-12).*

Sadly, this message of sacrifice for the Gospel is not heard often enough in America. Many in the church are moving farther away from God's Word and are embracing a theology of compromise that is powerless to sustain them and will cause them to forfeit that blessed place that Christ has prepared for His followers for eternity.

The good news is that it is not too late. Our condition is not our conclusion. Members of the church do not have to settle for a profession of faith that is limited to the corporate worship experience one day a week and living beneath the privileges of regenerated

Christians six days a week. We must believe that the church does not have to lie down and play dead in the hope that Satan will be placated if we allow sin to reign. No! That is unacceptable to the growth of the kingdom of God.

It is time for the church to reject the gods of popularity, conformity, acceptance, monetary gain, sexual immorality and all other sins that weaken the church's witness. We must reject all idols that distort the teachings of Jesus Christ. In many ways the church has drifted into idol worship. You ask, "How?" When we are more concerned about what people say about us than what God says, that is idol worship. When we compromise God's Word in order to receive a grant for a program or project, that is idol worship. When we allow persons in the church to lead because they have money, or because we are impressed with their talents, even though we know they are not living for God, that is idol worship. When we are more concerned about numerical growth in the church rather than spiritual growth that is idol worship. When we place more emphasis on fund raising than on making disciples and teaching the people how to live for God, that is idol worship. A reporter interviewed a preacher at a local church in Boston, Massachusetts. The reporter said the preacher was more concerned about money than spirituality. In speaking about his congregation, she quoted the preacher as saying, "They don't need to look at me on Sunday as long as they send their tithes." That is a sad commentary on the church.

If we are serious about impacting the world for

Christ, it requires that we move from a life of sin and complacency to a life of holiness, which is pleasing to God. We must first want to change our thinking and our lifestyle before we can change the world. Someone once said, "He (or she) that seeks to conquer the world must first conquer himself (or herself)." Why have we allowed Satan to distract us from the ways of God? We can all remember when we cried out to God to deliver us from a life of sin, and now many of us have lost sight of the holiness of God and are lusting after the ways of the world. Perhaps we should reflect on Paul's words to the church at Rome, *"But now that you have been set free from sin and have become slaves to God, the benefit you reap leads to holiness, and the result is eternal life"* (Rom. 6:22).

Oh, how quickly we forget about the blessings of God. How easy it is to become distracted and take God for granted. Paul reminded the Roman Christians that it was not long ago that they were slaves to sin; they were trapped by demons and were powerless to help themselves. In other words, Paul was saying that sin used to do more than influence them; it dominated their lives. Similarly, it once dominated our lives and forced us into areas that were far removed from God's laws. We were prisoners of sin, locked within our reality of shame and iniquity, without a key to escape. We could not bribe our way out, because Satan is the master of bribes. We could not lie our way out, because Satan is the father of lies. We did not have a high priest to let us out, because by our actions we had denied the

Lordship of Jesus Christ. We need to remember what a miserable state we were in before we were saved. Then one day we heard the good news of the Gospel and accepted Jesus Christ as our personal Lord and Savior, and our lives were transformed from a state of spiritual depravity, degradation, and depression, to a life of hope, peace, love, joy, contentment, faith and holiness. God calls us to live holy for Him.

> The Greek term in the New Testament for the concept of holiness is presented primarily by the adjectives "hagios," "hagiasmos," "hagiotes" and "hagiosyne;" and by the very "hagiazao," which means to make holy or sanctify. Of the three nouns only "hagiasmos"can be rendered as indicating the process of making holy, i.e., sanctification or consecration (Vine 307).

> "Hagiotes," personal holiness, indicates purity or ethical uprightness, the divine purity to which believers will ultimately be conformed, Heb. 12:10 (Ibid 307).

Many of us are intimidated by the term "holiness," but we don't have to be. Holiness simply speaks of Christian character and personal conduct. Character is built daily through personal integrity. Although it is not discussed much these days, Christian character develops one into the person God created him or her to be. It transforms our lives from seeking to please people and self, to seeking to please God. Our conduct flows from our character.

Our actions are determined by our internal thoughts, desires, and feelings inside of us. If we develop Christian character according to the Word of God, our hearts will be filled with agape love for humanity, we will be committed to live for God; and we will yearn to share with others what we learn. We will not intentionally hurt anyone's feelings or covet the possessions of others. Envy and jealousy will not reside in our spirits. We will have the strength and courage to say "no" to those things that are not pleasing to God. We will not use profanity, engage in violence, be mean-spirited or unforgiving, because the Holy Spirit within will encourage us to forsake all else and follow Jesus. Christian character requires confession and sacrifice. It impels us to declare to God, "Whatever I wanted or thought I wanted, I want you more. There is no one and nothing that I desire more than you, so I confess my sins before you Holy God and I thank you for forgiving me, and giving me a new beginning in You, in Jesus name. Amen." (1 Jn. 1:9). It is the recognition that once we were in bondage to sin, but now we are free unto righteousness. We are armed with the provisions of Calvary, the benefits of the Resurrection, and the power of the Holy Spirit. We no longer have to submit to sin. We are free from the law and live under grace; however, grace is not a license for us to go back into our former life of sin.

The challenge for us is to determine how we can grow spiritually when the world demands so much from us: our time, our money, our loyalty, our minds. In order to grow spiritually, we cannot buy into the secular model of success, which places value on a life of affluence by any means necessary, luxury at any cost, and sin without repentance. We live in the information age in which we are bombarded with a broad range of outside stimuli including telephones, cellular phones, email, the Internet, beepers, palm pilots, faxes, television, radio, ipods, mp3, DVDs, CDs, and other forms of media and entertainment, yet we must intentionally separate ourselves for a period of time daily and experience solitude as we thirst for and seek the quiet contemplative spiritual life of prayer, fasting and meditation. We must enter into that secret place with the Lord where we can commune with Him alone, and receive divine guidance and direction from God.

How are you spending your time? On a sheet of paper, draw a large circle, divide the amount of time you spend on the myriad of things you do each day, including time spent with God. Satan will do all that he can to prevent you from spending quality time with our Lord. He has devised a plot to prevent us (the church) from fulfilling God's purpose and to destroy our witness through the devices of distractions, disinterest, disillusion and disconnection.

Distractions are one of Satan's favorite ways to keep us from fulfilling God's purpose in our lives. Sometimes we may not be aware of the distractions, because they are so subtle:

- I don't have time for prayer and devotions; I know God will understand I am busy.

- Will this contact help me in my quest for power, status, and recognition?
- What's in it for me and mine?
- I need to devote more time to my relationship with my significant other if I want it to work, so that means I have less time for God. God will understand.
- Who will notice me? Who will praise me?
- I know what the Bible says, but God doesn't really expect us to live like that. After all, I am only human. I'll do this and repent later. God will understand.
- I know I am not supposed to date anyone who is not saved, but I really like this person and the person likes me, too.

Distractions can be deadly. How many times have we heard of persons involved in a car accident because they were distracted? They took their eyes off the road for just a second and caused a collision, sometimes a fatal collision. Distractions have the same effect within the church. They will cause us to lose our spiritual fervor and our desire to put God first. When we take our eyes off God for even a short period of time, we end up on a collision course with Satan, which could lead to spiritual and physical death. When we are too busy for God for whatever reason — career, travel, meetings, relationships, children, spouse, etc. — we are, indeed, TOO BUSY and we need to slow down.

We are also distracted by what I call "Meology." The term "meology," which I coined, means everything revolves around "me"— "I am the center of all things and the most important person in my sphere of influence." Do you know anyone like that? Unfortunately, meology is very prevalent in the church. Those who suffer from this affliction are always right; they love to be in charge; they tell everyone what to do, and they have a large following because of their status in the church or in the world. They become their own frame of reference and fail to acknowledge the authority of God's Word as the ultimate frame of reference. Consequently, they expect the church to follow their ways instead of the ways of God, and too often, since they have the skills to influence people, their way prevails. Too often we acquiesce to their demands. How sad it is that we allow ourselves to be distracted to the extent that we cannot spiritually discern the work of the evil one among us. James instructs us very clearly on this point:

> *Submit yourselves, then, to God. Resist the devil, and he will flee from you. Come near to God and he will come near to you. Wash your hands, you sinners, and purify your hearts, you double-minded. Grieve, mourn and wail. Change your laughter to mourning and your joy to gloom. Humble yourselves before the Lord, and He will lift you up.* (Jam. 4:7-10)

We are also distracted when we prefer to hear a clever story from the pulpit that entertains rather than the uncompromising Word of God that will strengthen us for life's journey. So often preachers have to condense the message to fit into the allotted timeslot. Preachers almost apologize for taking the congregation's time. Too often we preface our sermon with the remarks such as, "I won't be long"; "Let us look quickly at the text"; "In these few minutes that are mine"; and "Let me give my sermon text as I hasten to the benediction." There have been times in my ministry when I felt like I was on a treadmill, because the people were accustomed to a short sermon. I understand that time is limited when there is a special program in the church; however, when we come together as the Body of Christ in the Sunday corporate worship experience, we need to celebrate the preached word together and hear God's Word to His church that will build our faith and strengthen our witness. (I always wondered why time limits are not imposed on the collection of the offering). Let us not allow distractions to dilute our Christian witness and extinguish our spiritual fervor. When we give in to distractions, we can easily become disinterested.

To be "disinterested" is to have no interest in spiritual reflection. We do not want to take the time to learn the deeper things of God. Everything else seems more important. Disinterested persons are quick to say, "It doesn't take all that to be a Christian" or "You're a fanatic." But sadly, when we neglect a well-balanced diet of praise, prayer, Scripture reading, Bible study and worship, the Body of Christ suffers from spiritual malnutrition, and disinterest can lead to disillusion.

Disillusion occurs when the opinions of the world become more important to us than following biblical principles. There is a prevalent belief within the church that if we do what Satan wants but call it "tolerance," we can still say we are serving God. My friends, when that happens, rest assured we are in a state of disillusion. If we do not live a life grounded in Christology, and if we do not see the teachings of Jesus as paramount, we are in a state of disillusion. When the Church condones racism and sexism, be assured that the adversary has infiltrated our lives and the life of the Church. When distractions, disinterest and disillusion are present, we become disconnected to the vine and bear no fruit for the Kingdom of God (John 15). We lose our zeal for praise. We are more concerned about what time the service will end than we are about our commitment to worship God in the beauty of holiness.

Disconnection is a move away from God into a life of apostasy and sin. This sin — this straying away from God — does not happen all at once. It is usually an accumulation of concessions, compromises and indulgences. You might say to yourself,

- "Oh, I'll go there just this one time."
- "I'll do it just this one time."
- "I'll pretend that I did not hear that, or see that, just this one time."
- "I know it is wrong, but I'll agree with them, just this one time."

When we allow ourselves to be distracted from the truth of God's Word and the fellowship of the Holy Spirit, we yield ourselves piecemeal to sin, little by little, day by day, and before we know it, we have lost our spiritual passion, given up our freedom in Christ, and are once more slaves to sin. Remember, if Satan can somehow distract us, cause us to take our minds off of God, holy righteous living, and purity of heart for just a moment, we will find that our spiritual dedication to God will begin to dissipate. First, we will feel guilty, but each time we neglect our time with God or our attendance in His house of worship and give in to the demands of others or desires of our flesh, the guilt decreases, and it becomes easier and easier to neglect God. Sometimes the guilt is replaced by anger. Some may say, "Well, I'm doing the best I can." "I'm only human." "What do they expect from me?" "Give me a break." "I'm tired." And our guilt and anger begin to drown out the gentle, quiet voice of the Holy Spirit, who lives inside of us. This is very dangerous, because it could lead to a seared conscience. If that happens, we will not even hear the Holy Spirit anymore, because we have chosen to follow the voice of distractions rather than the voice of God. We will forfeit the divine direction and guidance of the Holy Spirit for the instant gratification of sin in order to be politically and socially correct. Then, when trouble comes or we feel unhappy, we begin to say, "Where is God?" "Why won't God tell me what to do?" "I can't hear God." But God has not moved away from us; we have moved away from God. It is time for us to wake up! This is spiritual warfare (Eph. 6:10-18). We have to fight back if we are going to be victorious over the sin of distractions.

We are living in evil, wicked times. The temptation of distractions is always before us. The battle between good and evil will intensify with each new day. God, however, has already given us a blueprint in His Word for us to resist Satan and stay focused on God. Paul warns Timothy of godlessness in the last days (2 Tim. 3:1-9) and against false teachers (1 Tim. 4:1; 2 Tim. 2:14). Paul informs the readers of this text that the last days have already begun. He prophesied through the Holy Spirit that the values of humankind would become grounded in principles of relativism and accommodationist rationalism as the end approaches (cf. 2 Pet. 3:3; 1 Jn. 2:18; Jude vv. 17-18). The last days would be marked by ever-increasing wickedness in the world, a collapse of moral standards, and an increase of false believers (2 Tim. 3). He describes the false teachers as evil, wicked, deceitful, cunning and crafty, and warns that the righteous must have nothing to do with them. Paul's words are instructive today, and in heeding them, we ought not associate with false teachers, attend their events, give donations or support their functions, or desire what they have, because their path leads only to trouble and total destruction.

This prophecy is being fulfilled in our lifetime. We are living in the last days, and we must be on guard against the evil of this world. We are the righteousness of God through Christ Jesus, and we must steer clear of trouble and titillating temptation. We must not flirt with it or believe that we can outwit the evil one. Satan has been on his job distracting people for a long time. We are not called to go toe-to-toe with him, but we are called to use our spiritual weapons to gain the victory:

> *For though we live in the world, we do not wage war as the world does. The weapons we fight with are not the weapons of the world. On the contrary, they have divine power to demolish strongholds. We demolish arguments and every pretension that sets itself up against the knowledge of God, and we take captive every thought to make it obedient to Christ.* (2 Cor. 10:3-5)

We cannot allow Satan to provoke us into a battle using his weapons – pride, power, might or material wealth. God has pre-determined the weapons that will guarantee us victory every time the evil one confronts us. We ought to memorize Second Corinthians 10:3-5 so that we are never without our arsenal of protection. When we fight back using God's weapons, the Holy Spirit will steer us away from every trap that is set for us and guide us to make decisions that are in accordance with the Word of God. We must be diligent in our fight against distractions in our personal lives and in the church universal.

We, the Body of Christ, must have the courage to live by God's holy Word seven days a week. How can we do this? We can do it when the church cries out to God for a fresh anointing of the power of the Holy Spirit and when we use our spiritual gifts. I believe that as Christians are baptized in the Holy Spirit and serve in the area of their spiritual gifts, we will see a reversal in the stagnation and decline that have penetrated many mainline denominations, and we will once again worship God in spirit and in truth, with the expectation of spending eternity with our Lord.

See it now through your spiritual eyes. Around the throne room of God is a crescendo of praise and worship rising as the assembled angelic hosts proclaim the holiness of God. Sometimes time constraints cause us to limit our praise and worship to God in church, but in Heaven there are no watches, no televisions, no computers, no sports - nothing to distract us from the praise and worship of our holy God whom we love and cherish with all of our hearts. In Heaven we will have the opportunity to say, "Thank You, Abba Father, for Your *agape* love. Thank You, Father, for protecting me from those things that I could not see. Thank You, Master, for taking care of my family, my loved ones and me. Thank You, Lord, most of all for Jesus Christ, who gave His life as a living sacrifice that my sins would be forgiven. He arose from the dead so that I could be justified with You. Father, I thank You for all of my blessings. I love You, I honor You, I cherish You, and I adore You because You, and You alone, are worthy of the praise." Oh, what a great day that will be when we can praise our God without restraints.

Every day I am striving to make Heaven my home. I am trying to live a little better today than I did yesterday. I am trying to love my sisters and brothers more today than I did yesterday. I am trying to die to the flesh so that I may live in the spirit daily. I want to live holy because God is holy. Like you, I have read in the Bible of God's majesty, God's splendor, God's beauty and God's shekeniah glory. The testimonies of the saints fill my heart with joy, but that alone is not enough for me. I want to see God for myself. I want to walk the streets paved with gold. I want to enter the pearly gates. I want to run to the throne room of God and join in with the living creatures as they give glory, honor and thanks to our God who sits on the throne and who lives and reigns forever and ever. I want to join in with the twenty-four elders as they fall down before God and lay their crowns before the throne and proclaim, *"You are worthy, our Lord and God, to receive glory and honor and power, for you created all things and by your will they were created and have their being"* (Rev. 4:11).

But most of all, I want to see JESUS, my Lord and Savior, who allowed me to come to Him in my broken condition and ministered healing to my soul. I want to tell Jesus that the journey was difficult, but because of His perfect love and empowerment of the Holy Spirit, I was able to defeat the sin of distractions and give my heart, body and soul to living holy for Him. I want to thank Jesus, because even when I stumbled and was less than perfect, He still loved me and provided a way of escape (1 Cor. 10:13).

Jesus did not allow Satan to snatch you or me out of His hands, and because He was not distracted en route to Calvary, we have the power to resist distractions in every area of our lives. Jesus has left a legacy for us. We can say "NO" to those things that are not aligned with the Word of God, even if it means being misunderstood by our denomination. If we stand firm for Jesus, He will stand with us and lead us to victory. We will defeat the sin of distractions when we purpose in our hearts to live for Jesus and refuse to compromise His Word. Then the church will regain its rightful place of leadership in the world. The church will set a godly example of how we "overcame Satan by the blood of the Lamb and the word of our testimony" (Rev. 12:11). Be strong. Be courageous and stand your ground for Jesus. We are winners in spiritual warfare, because Jesus has defeated Satan, sin and death. With Jesus, we have the victory now, and we can praise and worship our God throughout eternity.

Summary

Jesus has left us, His church, to occupy until He returns. We have the responsibility to use the mantle He has passed on to us to lead people back to God's holy Word. The church must be purged of its desire to run after and endorse any teaching that is in conflict with the inerrant Word of God. *"Stay away from those who have a form of godliness but deny its power. Have nothing to do with them"* (2 Tim. 3:5). It is not too late. We can renounce distractions and start to live holy for God today. We must be strong and courageous enough to say that unrepentant sin is not acceptable in God's house or in our homes, nor is it acceptable for those of us who are born-again Christians. We are obligated to separate ourselves from sin and relinquish spiritual, political, social and economic alliances that cause us to deny the

Lordship of Jesus Christ. The church must not give in to the sin of distractions. As we are led by Jesus and by the power of the Holy Spirit, we can set a righteous example for the world to follow. This is the mission <u>FOR THOSE WHO BELIEVE in the renewal of the church through the ministry of the Holy Spirit.</u>

<u>PRAYER</u>

(SACRIFICE)

Abba Father,

I exalt Your name and I thank You that we are not longer victims to the distractions of Satan. Through Jesus we shall continually offer you a sacrifice of praise – the fruit of our lips that confess Your name. In Jesus' name we pray. Amen. (Heb. 13:15).

The next chapter will focus on the person and the work of the Holy Spirit as recorded in Holy Scripture.

CHAPTER 3

THE CONVICTION

*"You will receive power when the
Holy Spirit comes on you."*
(Acts 1:8)

There is one God who exists eternally in three persons: God the Father, God the Son and God the Holy Spirit. Christians are well versed in the doctrine of God the Father and God the Son; however, many regenerated, born-again Christians have not studied the work of the third person of the Trinity, God the Holy Spirit. For centuries there has been a paucity of teaching on the importance of the ministry of the Holy Spirit in general and the baptism in the Holy Spirit and gifts of the Holy Spirit in particular. The United States did not witness a resurgence of these tenets until the twentieth century.

The scarcity of teaching on the baptism in the Holy Spirit and spiritual gifts has caused believers to live beneath our privileges and impeded our spiritual growth. Many mainline denominations have experienced a decline in their membership largely because parishioners have not been taught how to receive the baptism in the Holy Spirit, which empowers us to live consecrated lives before God. The Holy Spirit gives us spiritual boldness to resist the temptation to compromise the Word of God. If the church is to reverse the downward spiral in church membership, take its rightful place of leadership in the world, fulfill the Great Commission, experience joy in serving and be on the cutting edge of effecting change in the world, we need to be renewed by the power of the Holy Spirit.

Who is the Holy Spirit?

The Holy Spirit is the third person of the Godhead. He is pre-existent with the Father and the Son. He was with the Father and the Son in the beginning. The Word of God says, *"In the beginning God created the heavens and the earth. Now the earth was formless and empty, darkness was over the surface of the deep, and the Spirit of God was hovering over the waters"* (Gen. 1:1-2). The Holy Spirit is the "dynamis" (power) of the Holy Trinity, but He does not do anything on His own. The Holy Spirit carries out the will of God the Father that comes through Jesus Christ, God the Son. Jesus said, *He (the Holy Spirit) will not speak on his own; he will speak only what he hears, and he will tell you what is yet to come"* (John 16:13). Even though God the Father, God the Son and God the Holy Spirit are one

God manifested in three persons, the leadership is based on their predetermined roles, always in order and harmony.

Look at the creation of heaven and earth (Gen. 1). As God the Holy Trinity looked upon the vast emptiness and darkness that covered the earth, God the Father decided that the time had come to create earth, humankind, nature and animals. God the Son and God the Holy Spirit were in position to receive the command from God the Father. So when God the Father spoke that powerful, immortal word, **"LET,"** the miraculous occurred:

- "Let there be light, and there was light" (1:3).

- "Let there be an expanse between the waters to separate water from water . . . And it was so" (1:6-7).

- "Let the water under the sky be gathered to one place, and let dry ground appear. And it was so." (1:9).

- "Let the land produce vegetation . . . And it was so" (1:11).

- "Let there be lights in the expanse of the sky to separate the day from the night...and it was so" (1:14-15).

- "Let the water teem with living creatures, and let birds fly above the earth . . . And God saw that it was good" (1:20- 21).

- "Let the land produce living creatures according to their kinds . . . And it was so" (1:24).

- "Let us make man in our image, in our likeness . . . So God created man in his own image, in the image of God he created him; male and female he created them" (1:26- 27).

In saying, "Let," God the Father was giving His sovereign permission for God the Son and God the Holy Spirit to move into action. At the sound of the word "Let," the pre-incarnate Jesus Christ, God the Son, who is the logos (word) of God, was the "let" that was spoken over the creation process. God the Holy Spirit was hovering over the earth, waiting for the command to energize the elements with His supreme power. Although the Holy Spirit could have brought the elements together while hovering over the earth, He waited for the command to come from God the Father and be given to Him through God the Son, because the Holy Spirit only speaks and moves on what He hears from the Son, which comes directly from the Father. In other words, the order established by the Trinity is never broken; and the predetermined roles of the Trinity are never compromised.

The Attributes of the Holy Spirit

The Holy Spirit possesses the attributes of the Triune God. He is omnipresent, omniscient and omnipotent.

The Holy Spirit is omnipresent. There is nowhere we can go to flee from His presence. He is everywhere at the same time. David said, *"Where can I go from your Spirit? Where can I flee from your presence? If I go up to the heavens, you are there; if I make my bed in the depths, you are there"* (Ps. 139:7-8).

Before I made a full commitment to Jesus Christ, Psalm 139 was very frightening to me. I wanted God to see me on Sunday in the worship service, but I did not want God to see me when I socialized in ways that did not bring glory to His name. I felt convicted and I tried to pass over that chapter every time I read through the book of Psalms. I could feel the Holy Spirit tugging at my heart, imploring me to change my life, to make a total commitment to Jesus. The words resounded in my spirit – God is omnipresent. He is everywhere at the same time. I began to think, "If I am ashamed for God to see me here, then I should not be here. If I am ashamed for God to see me with them, then I should not be with them. If I am ashamed for God to see me doing these things, then I should not do these things." I knew that I had to make a decision. I had to decide what was most important to me. I reflected on my lifestyle and realized that nothing was more important to me than living a holy life. I wanted to enjoy the privilege of reading God's Word in its entirety, without skipping over Psalm 139. Once I made a full commitment to Jesus, Psalm 139 gave me the peace and assurance to know that God is indeed everywhere at the same time. That means no weapon formed against me or any of God's children will prosper (Isa. 54:17). God the Holy Spirit will protect us from dangers seen and unseen. The Holy Spirit is our comforter and companion every day, twenty-four hours a day.

The Holy Spirit is omniscient. He knows all things (Ps. 139:1-6; 147:5). His knowledge embraces infinity and spans eternity. Paul wrote,

> *...The Spirit searches all things, even the deep things of God. For who among men knows the thoughts of a man except the man's spirit within him? In the same way no one knows the thoughts of God except the Spirit of God.* (1 Cor. 2:10-11)

This is true even in our personal lives. When we think that no one knows what we are going through, our hurt, our pain and our frustrations or secret desires, the Holy Spirit knows and the Holy Spirit cares. He is concerned about whatever concerns us. He is our comforter; the one we can go to when we are wounded or broken, knowing that He will not mistreat us or harm us in any way. We must never feel ashamed when the burdens of our heart cause us to cry out to God for help. You see, God, the Holy Spirit, already knows what we are going through. When we cannot articulate our feelings, the Holy Spirit within knows our heart. The Holy Spirit is omniscient and He intercedes on our behalf to the Father even when our conscious minds cannot think of words to say (Rom. 8:26-27).

Have you ever been in a place in your life when you were hurting too much to pray an eloquent prayer? I can remember fourteen years ago I filed for divorce. I had not planned to seek a divorce, but I found out some disturbing news that made it impossible for me to continue in the marriage. There was no question in my mind about the path I had to take. I knew the marriage had to end, but what I did not know was how I was going to support my two daughters (Frances was 19 and Gabriella was 4) and myself. I had been a full-time student for the past four years and had just completed my Master of Divinity. I had not worked outside of the home for several years. Consequently, I did not have any money or assets in my name, and there was no one who could loan me a large sum of money to tide us over for an extended period of time. I remember one night shortly after the separation, Frances, Gabriella and I were sitting in bed together, and Frances, who was a sophomore in college at that time, asked me, "Mommy, what are we going to do?" Oh, how those words pierced my heart, because I did not have a short-range or long-range plan for us to follow. The condition in which we found ourselves was as much a shock to me as it was to them, and so I responded, "I don't know, baby, but God will help us." I got down on my knees and I cried out to God in my despair. I cannot remember the entire prayer, but I do remember saying, "Dear God, I have taught my daughters to love you, to trust you, and to go to you whenever they have a problem. I have taught them that you will never leave us or forsake us and that you will provide for all of our needs. God, we need your help right now. Please help us and make a way for us." I experienced such intense heartache that

I couldn't worry about praying "properly." All I could do was fall on my face before God, cry from the depths of my soul, and ask God to help us, to have mercy on us, and to take the pain away. I could not dress it up; I could not write it on paper; I could not seek the opinion of others about how I should approach God. No, I knew I had to petition God for my children and myself. I knew I had to have an immediate audience with God because the weight was too heavy for me to carry. God heard my prayers, and God provided abundant blessings for us through the power of the Holy Spirit and the loving kindness of our church family. All of our needs were met. Hallelujah!

The Holy Spirit is omnipotent. He has all power and authority to do all things (Ps. 147:13-18; Jer. 32:17; Mt. 19:26; Lk. 1:37). He is eternal. From everlasting to everlasting, He is God (Ps. 90:1-2; 102:12; Is. 57:15). There has never been a time when God the Holy Spirit did not exist in the past or present, neither will there be a time in the future without Him.

The Holy Spirit is infinitely perfect, holy and good. When David confessed his sin before God, his prayer was, *"Do not cast me from your presence or take your Holy Spirit from me"* (Ps. 51:11). David knew the goodness of the Spirit of God, and he prayed, *"Teach me to do your will, for you are my God; may your good Spirit lead me on level ground"* (Ps. 143:10). We need not worry about defeat when we follow the leading of the Holy Spirit. There is no power on earth or under the earth that can compare with the all-surpassing power of the Holy Spirit.

Therefore, it is important that we train our spirits to be quiet and listen for the still, quiet voice of the Holy Spirit. We will be victorious when we let the Holy Spirit establish the time and the method for us to proceed in every area of our lives.

The Holy Spirit is the fountain-spring of truth and goodness. He is without sin and absolutely holy. John declared, *"Who will not fear you, O Lord, and bring glory to your name? For you alone are holy. All nations will come and worship before you, for your righteous acts have been revealed"* (Rev. 15:4).

The Personality of the Holy Spirit

People often refer to the Holy Spirit as an "it" or a "force," but Scripture reveals that the Holy Spirit is a "person." Jesus gave the Holy Spirit personal names: "counselor" (John. 14:16) and "the Spirit of Truth" (John. 14:17). Moreover, Jesus used personal pronouns when speaking of the Holy Spirit (John. 16:8,13-14).

In his book The Holy Spirit, Edward Bickersteth cites additional Scriptural references to authenticate the personhood of the Holy Spirit:

> The Holy Spirit possesses such qualities as a person only can possess: intelligence, affection and will. Scripture testifies of:

- The knowledge of the Spirit (1 Cor. 2:10,11).
- The Divine love of the Spirit (Rom. 15:30; 12:1; and 5:5).

- The self-determining will of the Spirit (John. 6:38).

The Holy Spirit performs such actions
as only a person can perform:

- He created the worlds and gives life to those who live (Ps. 33:6)
- He convicts the world of sin, righteousness and judgment (Gen. 6:3; John. 16:8; Ezek. 12:7-11).
- He performs miracles (Acts 2:4; 8:39; Rom. 15:19).
- He caused the Virgin Mary to conceive (Luke 1:35).
- He inspired the sacred writers (2 Pet. 1:21).
- He appoints ministers in the Church (Acts 20:28).
- He intercedes for us in prayer (Rom. 8:26).
- He teaches, and comforts, and guides us into all truth (John 14:26, 16:13).

The Holy Spirit is capable of suffering
injuries as only a person can suffer:

- He can be vexed (Isa. 63:10).
- He can be grieved (Eph. 4:30; 1 Thess. 5:19).
- He can be blasphemed (Matt. 12:31; Mark 3:29; Acts 5:3, 9).
- He can be lied against and tempted (Mark 3:29).
- He can be insulted (Acts 7:51) (Bickertsteth 41-44)

The Holy Spirit is the Third Person of the Godhead, not a Hollywood creation of "the force."

The Old Testament Witness of the Holy Spirit

The Old Testament and the New Testament are replete with references to the person and work of the Holy Spirit. In the Old Testament, the Holy Spirit came upon prophets and inspired them to proclaim the word of the Lord. They boldly communicated accurately the messages they received from the Spirit (Num. 11:29; 1 Sam. 10:5-6, 10; 2 Chron. 20:14; 24:19-20; Neh. 9:30; Isa. 61:1-3; Mic. 3:8; Zech. 7:12). Sometimes preachers today do not want to deliver the word the Holy Spirit has placed in our hearts because it may cause controversy or sound too fundamental. But Old Testament prophets who spoke the word of God powerfully encourage us. They were willing to die for their faith in God, because they trusted the God who was not seen more than they feared humans who were seen. Many of those great saints of old are listed in the faith chapter of Hebrews 11. They risked their lives to proclaim the Word of God. How much more then are we convicted to follow the voice of the Holy Spirit in this present age when the only negative consequences (in America) may be the disapproval of society or loss of membership in inter-faith organizations that do not recognize the deity of Jesus Christ. We must be bold and determined to proclaim, "Thus saith the Lord." We do not have to be super humans to confess our faith; we only have to be willing to be led by the power of the Holy Spirit. God will equip us to proclaim the Gospel message. Let us take our eyes off the world, self, and self-imposed limitations and look through spiritual eyes at the infinite power of God to perfect those things that concern us and empower us to speak God's Word with authority. We can learn from ordinary saints of old who refused to compromise God's Word.

Moses was an ordinary man until he had an encounter with God on Mount Moriah. God spoke to him from a burning bush and gave him the charge to lead the children of Israel out of Egypt. Moses, like many of us, resisted at first because when he looked at himself in the natural, he knew that he could not stand against Pharaoh and the Egyptian army. He immediately assessed his credentials and told God that he was not the man for the job. In fact, he noted that he did not even speak clearly. Similarly, we often look at ourselves through human lens rather than spiritual lens. We are quick to focus on what we do not have and what we cannot do rather than looking to God who is *"able to do immeasurably more than all we ask or imagine, according to his power that is at work within us"* (Eph. 3:20). If we are going to offer biblical leadership, we must believe in the supernatural power of the Holy Spirit and walk where and how He directs us.

When Moses took his eyes off his human limitations and placed his eyes on God, the Creator and sustainer of the universe, his life was transformed. He moved to a new level of faith, and the Holy Spirit equipped him to fulfill God's call on his life. Moses always sought God's instructions and wisdom before leading the Israelites, and God responded by anointing him with the power to lead the people by the Holy Spirit. When the Israelites complained about not having meat to eat, Moses cried out to the Lord, because the responsibility of leading that vast number of men plus women and children (Ex. 12:37) became too burdensome for him. The Lord said to Moses:

> *Bring me seventy of Israel's elders who are known to you as leaders and officials among the people. Have them come to the Tent of Meeting, that they may stand there with you. I will come down and speak with you there, and I will take of the Spirit that is on you and put the Spirit on them. They will help you carry the burden of the people so that you will not have to carry it alone.* (Num. 11:16-17)

The purpose of God's Spirit coming upon men and women in the Old Testament was to equip them for leadership (cf. Joshua [Num. 27:18]; Deborah [Jgs. 4]; Gideon [Jgs. 6:34]; David [1 Sam. 16:13] and Zerubbabel [Zec. 4:6]). We learn at least three lessons from their lives: 1) God is the giver of the gifts; 2) God lifts the burden if it is too much for us to bear; and 3) God will give us the right spirit to perform the tasks He wants us to do.

In the Old Testament the Holy Spirit came upon a person or persons at a particular time to enable them to fulfill various acts of service to God, but there was not a great outpouring on all the people.

The Old Testament pointed the way to the New Covenant established in the New Testament by the atonement of Jesus Christ. The age of the Holy Spirit began ten days after Jesus' ascension, and will continue until the Parousia of Jesus Christ.

Isaiah prophesied about the Messiah and the work of the Spirit:

> *A shoot will come up from the stump of Jesse; from his roots a Branch will bear fruit. The Spirit of the Lord will rest on him – the Spirit of wisdom and of understanding, the Spirit of counsel and of power, the Spirit of knowledge and of the fear of the Lord—and he will delight in the fear of the Lord.* (Isa. 11:1-2)

Isaiah prophesied more than seven hundred years before the incarnation of Jesus Christ, for he foresaw the coming of the Messiah filled with the power and anointing of the Holy Spirit. He proclaimed:

> *The Spirit of the Sovereign Lord is on me, because the Lord has anointed me to preach good news to the poor. He has sent me to bind up the brokenhearted, to proclaim freedom for the captives and release from darkness for the prisoners, to proclaim the year of the Lord's favor and the day of vengeance of our God, to comfort all who mourn, and provide for those who grieve in Zion – to bestow on them a crown of beauty instead of ashes, the oil of gladness instead of mourning, and a garment of praise*

instead of a spirit of despair. They will be called oaks of righteousness, a planting of the Lord for the display of his splendor. (Isa. 61:1-3)

This Scripture was fulfilled in the New Testament. After John baptized Jesus, the Holy Spirit descended on Him in the form of a dove and led Jesus into the wilderness where Satan tempted Him for forty days and nights. After Jesus defeated Satan, He returned to Galilee in the power of the Spirit and went into the synagogue. When He was handed the scroll of Isaiah, He read from Isaiah 61:1,2 and He declared, *"Today this scripture is fulfilled in your hearing"* (Luke 4:21).

Other Old Testament passages of Scripture also point to the age of the Spirit (Isa. 32:15-17; 44:3-5; 59:20-21; Eze. 11:19-20; 36:26-27; 37:14; 39:29).

The New Testament Witness of the Holy Spirit

Jesus was conceived by the Holy Spirit. The angel Gabriel said to Mary, *"The Holy Spirit will come upon you, and the power of the Most High will overshadow you. So the holy one to be born will be called the Son of God"* (Lk. 1:35). In <u>The Full Life Bible</u>, Donald Stamps cites thirteen other examples of the Holy Spirit's relation to Jesus Christ:

1. He was filled with the Spirit (Matt. 3:16-17; Mark 1:12-13).
2. Preached in the Spirit (Luke 4:16-27).
3. Performed miracles by the power of the

Spirit (Matt. 12:28; Luke 11:20; Acts 10:38).

4. Will baptize believers in the Holy Spirit (Matt. 3:11; Mark 1:8; Acts 1:4-5; 11:16).
5. Promises the Holy Spirit as the counselor (John 14:16; 15:26-27; 16:7-15).
6. Promises the ministry of the Holy Spirit to flow through believers (John 7:37-39).
7. Is revealed to believers by the Spirit (John 16:13-15).
8. Offered Himself on the cross through the Spirit (Heb. 9:14).
9. Was raised from the dead by the Spirit (1 Cor. 15:2- 4).
10. Received the Spirit from the Father (John 16:4-14; Acts 2:33).
11. Poured out the Spirit upon believers (Acts 2:33; 38-39).
12. Is glorified by the Spirit (John 16:13-14).
13. The Spirit prays for His return (Rev. 22:17). (Stamps 1803)

In the Old Testament, the Holy Spirit came upon a person for a specific purpose, for a limited time, but in the New Testament, Jesus has sent Him to live in the hearts of all regenerated Christians (1 Cor. 6:19). The Holy Spirit brings glory to the Son as the Son glorifies the Father. He does not speak on His own; He speaks only what He hears, and He informs believers of things that will come to pass. He leads and guides the church into all truth. He brings the church together in unity (Eph.4:4); He empowers the church to witness for Christ (Acts 4:30-33; 1 Cor.

12:7-13; 14:1-33). He protects the church against false teachers (2 Tim. 1:14) and warns of apostasy (1 Tim. 4:1). He is the one who equips the church for spiritual warfare (Eph. 6:10-18). He always promotes righteousness (Eph. 2:21-22; 3:16-21; 1 Thess. 4:7-8).

The ministry of the Holy Spirit embraces every aspect of Christian life. He sanctifies and empowers believers for service by baptizing us in His Spirit (Acts 1:5; 1 Cor. 12:13), and He gives spiritual gifts to all believers (1 Cor. 12).

The Baptism in the Holy Spirit

The baptism in the Holy Spirit is distinct from water baptism and is available to all regenerated Christians. John the Baptist stated clearly, *"I baptize you with water for repentance. But after me will come one who is more powerful than I, whose sandals I am not fit to carry. He will baptize you with the Holy Spirit and with fire"* (Matt. 3:11; cf., Mk. 1:8; Lk. 3:16; Jn. 1:33). John prophesied about Jesus Christ, who alone has the power and the authority to baptize believers in the Holy Spirit.

After the resurrection, Jesus remained on the earth for forty days during which time He appeared to His disciples. On one occasion, just before His ascension, Jesus commanded them to stay in Jerusalem until they received the gift of the Father. He confirmed the prophecy of John the Baptist when He stated, *"John baptized with water, but in a few days you will be baptized with the Holy Spirit"* (Acts 1:5). Jesus knew that the disciples needed to be baptized in the Holy Spirit to carry out the Great Commission (Matt. 28:19-20). He knew they would be engaged in spiritual warfare *"against the powers of this dark world and against the spiritual forces of evil in the heavenly realms"* (Eph. 6:12), and human wisdom was inadequate to assure victory. Even though His work was finished and He was returning to the Father, Jesus, the Good Shepherd, never stopped caring for His sheep. He would not leave them defenseless against Satan. Jesus' final words to them were, *"But you will receive power when the Holy Spirit comes on you; and you will be my witnesses in Jerusalem, and in all Judea and Samaria, and to the ends of the earth"* (Acts 1:8). After Jesus gave them the promise of this special gift, He ascended into heaven. As the disciples stood there looking up, two angels appeared and encouraged their hearts saying, *"This same Jesus, who has been taken from you into heaven, will come back in the same way you have seen him go into heaven"* (Acts 1:11). And so, with this assurance, in obedience to Jesus, the men and women returned to Jerusalem where they gathered for worship, prayer and fasting. They did not have to wait long for Jesus to fulfill His promise.

The Baptism in the Holy Spirit at Pentecost and Today

Ten days after His ascension, Jesus sent the gift of the baptism in the Holy Spirit as the 120 men and women were worshiping God:

And when the day of Pentecost was fully come, they were all with one accord in one place. And suddenly there came a sound from heaven as of a rushing mighty wind, and it filled all the house where they were sitting. And there appeared unto them cloven tongues like as of fire, and it sat upon each of them. And they were all filled with the Holy Ghost, and began to speak with other tongues, as the Spirit gave them utterance. (Acts 2:1-4 KJV)

During this time, God-fearing Jews were in Jerusalem from every nation to celebrate the Feast of Pentecost. The Jews celebrated three great feasts, when all the males had to travel to Jerusalem: (1) The Feast of Unleavened Bread (Passover), which commemorated their divine deliverance from Egypt; (2) The Feast of Tabernacles, which commemorated their 40-year pilgrimage in the desert, with no permanent dwelling place; and (3) The Feast of Pentecost, which commemorated God giving the law to Moses at Mount Sinai. It was also called The Feast of Weeks and First Fruits, because the first fruits of the harvest were presented to God. It was fitting that the church would be established on this day because the feast was a celebration of harvest. Under the Old Dispensation, the people offered God the first fruits of the harvest. Now, under the New Dispensation, with the baptism in the Holy Spirit and the establishment of the New Testament Church, the people would offer unto God not a harvest of first fruits, but a harvest of souls for the Kingdom of God, through the proclamation of the

Gospel of Jesus Christ.

Charles W. Carter, Chairman and General Editor of The Wesleyan Bible Commentary, used four words to summarize the baptism in the Holy Spirit: power, purity, possession and proclamation (Carter 504), and I would like to add a fifth word, praise.

Power: Divine power came like a mighty rushing wind. The Greek word for spirit is *pneuma,* which means "wind" or "breath." The wind is invisible and cannot be controlled by any human being. Jesus said, *"The wind blows wherever it pleases. You hear its sound, but you cannot tell where it comes from or where it is going. So it is with everyone born of the Spirit"* (John 3:8). Just as the wind is invisible, so is the Spirit. Humans cannot control the wind, and they cannot control the Holy Spirit. He is supreme!

He came as a mighty rushing wind. Mighty speaks of power. The Spirit, who came to give them power to witness and to live a sanctified life, is all-powerful in Himself. He rushed in to empower His people! Rushing speaks of the approach. It is the divine action of the Spirit, coming from above, to help believers who are committed to Christ. The Holy Spirit is the wind and the breath of the almighty God. He is the manifestation of the divine presence and power of God on earth, and He graciously baptizes believers to endue us with power for witness and ministry.

Purity: Cloven tongues, like as of fire, rested on each of them. Fire was the fulfillment of the prophecy of John the Baptist, that Jesus would baptize believers with the Holy Spirit and with fire (Matt. 3:11; Mark 1:7-8). The fire was for purification. The fire of the

Holy Spirit cleanses the heart and thoughts of a person. He sanctifies believers. The fire of the Holy Spirit touches us, consumes all the impurities in our heart, and purges believers of all ungodly ways. The fire burns and destroys everything in our heart that does not conform to the will of God. Fire brings heat. The heat of the Holy Spirit changes a cold person into a person who is excited about Jesus. God does not want a cold church. He wants a church that is on fire for Him by the power and purity of the Holy Spirit. Jesus is pleased with believers who will sing His praises and witness to His saving power with boldness.

Possession: All of the believers at Pentecost were filled with the Holy Spirit. It was a personal filling for every believer. The Holy Spirit went into the recesses of every person's personality, stimulating every part of their being with the truth of God's word.

Every believer should desire to possess the baptism and thirst for it and keep praying until they receive it. Thirst for it, and don't let anyone tell you that you can't have the baptism. If you are a born again believer, you need the baptism in the Holy Spirit to empower you to live for Jesus. Thirst for it as you thirst for water. Water is a symbol of the Holy Spirit. You can't live without clean water in the natural, and you shouldn't live without the baptism in the spiritual. The Holy Spirit is living water, and only He can quench our spiritual thirst and satisfy the longings of our heart. Jesus said to the woman of Samaria that everyone who drinks this water (natural water) will be thirsty again, but the one who drinks the water He gives would never thirst. Indeed the water that Jesus gives believers will become in them a spring of water welling up to eternal life (Jn. 4:13 paraphrased). That is the baptism in the Holy Spirit!

Proclamation: The believers began to speak in other tongues as the Spirit enabled them. Speaking in tongues was an initial sign of the baptism in the Holy Spirit. They spoke in foreign languages that they had not studied, as well as in tongues of angels (1 Cor. 13:1). Tongues are not just for the Pentecostal church. Tongues are for all believers. There are two types of tongues: a prayer language (Rom. 8:26-27) and the gift of tongues (1 Cor. 12:10).

The first type of tongues is a prayer language. I believe God will give all believers a prayer language, because sometimes our vocabulary fails to express the true desire of our heart in prayer. We may find ourselves praying the same prayer over and over again out of habit, or because we don't know any other way to pray. But sometimes the circumstances of life can weigh so heavily upon us that we don't have time to recite an elegant prayer, nor do we have time to remember the ACTS (Adoration, Confession, Thanksgiving, and Supplication) acronym. All we know is that we need to commune with God immediately and share the burden of our heart. Scripture says,

> *The Spirit helps us in our weakness. We do not know what we ought to pray for, but the Spirit himself intercedes for us with groans that words cannot express. And he who searches our hearts knows the mind of the Spirit, because the Spirit*

intercedes for the saints in accordance with God's will. (Rom. 8:26-27)

The second type of tongues is the gift of tongues. The Holy Spirit decides who will receive this gift. Scripture says,

Now to each one the manifestation of the Spirit is given for the common good . . . to another speaking in different kinds of tongues, and to still another the interpretation of tongues. All these are the work of one and the same Spirit, and he gives them to each one, just as he determines. (1 Cor. 12:7, 10-11)

Scripture also gives instruction on the correct way to use tongues in the corporate worship experience:

If anyone speaks in a tongue, two – or at the most three —should speak, one at a time, and someone must interpret. If there is no interpreter, the speaker should keep quiet in the church and speak to himself and God. (1 Cor. 14:27-28)

Praise: Once these believers received the baptism in the Holy Spirit, they were no longer the same. They experienced an inner transformation; their hearts were changed. The Holy Spirit spoke through Ezekiel: *"I will give them an undivided heart and put a new spirit in them; I will remove from them their heart of stone and give them a heart of flesh. Then they will follow my decrees, and be careful to keep my laws. They will be my people, and I will be their God" (Ezek. 11:19-20).* I believe they praised God with all their heart, because once they received the baptism, they were no longer the same. They became bold and courageous and testified to the name of Jesus, and 3,000 persons were added to the Church that day. And the Baptism in the Holy Spirit is available to all believers today.

When you receive the Baptism in the Holy Spirit, you won't be up one day and down the next day. The Holy Spirit will bring stability to your life and transform you:

- From fear to faith
- From ignorance to informative
- From self-righteousness to self- sacrificing
- From doubt to determined
- From confused to certainty
- From cowardly to courageous
- From stressed to strength
- From belittled to beloved
- From hurt to hope
- From ridicule to respect
- From reluctant to resolute
- From weak to wise
- From exhausted to encouraged
- From powerless to powerful

You will be steady for Jesus and will serve Jesus in season and out of season. You will get tired, but you won't quit, because the Holy Spirit will empower you to keep trying until you are victorious. However, you must be born again (like the saints in the upper room on the day of Pentecost), before you can receive the baptism in the Holy Spirit.

Regeneration and baptism in the Holy Spirit are two separate experiences (Eph. 1:13; Acts 19:1-6). David Yonggi Cho affirms,

> Regeneration is the experience of receiving the life of the Lord by being grafted into the body of Christ through the Holy Spirit and the Scriptures. The baptism of the Holy Spirit is the experience in which Jesus fills believers with the power of God for ministry, service and victorious living.
>
> Regeneration grants a person everlasting life, while the baptism of the Holy Spirit grants regenerate believers the power of God to preach Christ (Cho 103).

The Gentile Believers Received the Baptism in the Holy Spirit in Samaria

After the martyrdom of Stephen, the church in Jerusalem suffered persecution. All of the believers, except the apostles, left Jerusalem and were scattered throughout Judea and Samaria. Philip, who had served as a deacon with Stephen, went down to Samaria and preached Christ. He was filled with the Holy Spirit and the zeal to witness for Jesus. Philip proclaimed with certainty that Jesus is the Christ, the Messiah, the Savior of the world, and his message was accompanied with great miracles, signs and wonders. The Gentiles listened and believed in the Lord Jesus Christ. After their confession of faith, Philip baptized them with water.

Upon hearing the news of the Gentile conversions, the apostles in Jerusalem immediately sent Peter and John to Samaria to visit the new believers. When they arrived, they did not question the authenticity of their conversion. They went to Samaria with the right attitude and filled with the Spirit. They knew that the believers had been baptized with water, and now they prayed that they would be baptized in the Holy Spirit. After praying, Peter and John laid hands on the believers and they received the Holy Spirit (Acts 8:5-13). Regeneration preceded the baptism in the Holy Spirit; they were two distinctly different experiences.

The Gentile Believers Received the Baptism in the Holy Spirit in Caesarea

God spread the flame of His Spirit throughout the Gentile world. In Acts 10, Scripture records that Cornelius and his household received the Holy Spirit. Cornelius lived in Caesarea. He was a centurion and a godly man. He was generous to the needy and prayed to God regularly. God was pleased with his sacrifices and his life and sent an angel to speak to him in a vision. *"Your prayers and gifts to the poor have come up as a memorial offering before God. Now send men to Joppa to bring back a man named Simon who is called Peter"* (Acts 10:4-5).

Cornelius obeyed and sent men to seek Peter. It is interesting that he did not ask the angel the purpose of Peter's visit to his home. He simply obeyed the Lord. As God spoke to Cornelius in a vision, He also spoke to Peter in a vision the next day. Prior to the vision, Peter had followed Jewish dietary laws that forbade him to eat pork. Also he and the Jews did not associate with Gentiles. However, through the vision, God showed him that He is the God of all people, Jew and Gentile alike, and that Peter must follow God, and not the Jewish tradition (Acts 10:9-23). On that day, God delivered Peter from racial bigotry. When the men arrived from Cornelius, Peter's heart was open to receive them, and he agreed to return to Caesarea with them the next day.

Cornelius did not doubt that Peter would come, because he trusted the God who instructed him to send for Peter. When Peter and the men arrived at Cornelius' home, they found a large audience waiting for them. Cornelius was so certain that Peter would come that he had invited his friends, relatives and neighbors to hear the Good News of the Gospel.

The first thing Peter did was to confess his sin of racism. *"I now realize how true it is that God does not show favoritism but accepts men from every nation who fear him and do what is right"* (Acts 10: 34-35). Peter repented because of the leading of the Holy Spirit who lived within him. Jesus said that the Holy Spirit would lead and guide believers into all truth for He is the Spirit of truth. Peter did not want to grieve the Holy Spirit with his carnal ways, so he humbled himself before the Lord and accepted the

Gentiles as equals, co-laborers for the Gospel of Jesus Christ.

While Peter was preaching the Gospel, the Holy Spirit fell on all the people and they spoke in other tongues and praised God. Peter, led by the Holy Spirit, baptized them because they had received the Holy Spirit just as the Jews had. You may ask, "How could they receive the baptism in the Spirit without first verbally accepting Jesus Christ as their Lord and Savior?" Although Scripture does not record their conversion, I believe that as Peter was preaching, they gave their hearts to Jesus.

Sometime later, Peter appeared before the Jerusalem Council in defense of the Gentiles. He attested that they had received the Holy Spirit as the Jews did on the day of Pentecost: *"God, who knows the heart, showed that he accepted them by giving the Holy Spirit to them, just as he did to us. He made no distinction between us and them, for he purified their hearts by faith"* (Acts 15:8-9). The hearts of the apostles had been purified as they prayed together in the upper room on the day of Pentecost. Now, the hearts of the Gentiles were purified as Peter preached Jesus to them at Cornelius' home, which confirmed that the same God gives His Spirit to all who believe by faith in the Lord Jesus Christ.

More Disciples Received the Baptism in the Holy Spirit in Ephesus

Church growth continued. God used the apostles, including Paul (read about his conversion and bap-

tism experience in Acts 9) to preach the Good News
of the Kingdom of God, and signs and wonders
accompanied their preaching.

Paul traveled extensively on three missionary
journeys witnessing for Jesus and planting churches.
On his third missionary journey, he visited Ephesus
and found some disciples. He asked them if they had
received the Holy Spirit. These disciples had not
even heard of the Holy Spirit; they had only received
the baptism of John for the repentance of sins. Paul
spoke the word to them, and they believed and were
baptized in the name of Jesus. Paul then laid hands
on them, and they were baptized in the Holy Spirit
and spoke in tongues (Acts 19:1-6).

Cho contends that before the church at Ephesus
received the baptism in the Holy Spirit, they were
weak and powerless. However, after they received
the Holy Spirit, a wonderful vitality and power of
faith exploded in their midst. After a while it became
a famous church that filled all of Asia Minor with the
Word of God.

The Book of Acts records many references to the
ministry of the Holy Spirit. It shows conclusively that
once believers received the baptism in the Holy
Spirit, they were empowered to live holy lives for
God and to witness with boldness for Jesus Christ.
Believers were persecuted for their faith; many were
martyred, but they refused to renounce Jesus Christ
as Lord and Savior. During the time of great persecution, the church grew at a phenomenal rate. The people had a great love for God and the courage of their
convictions (we need that love and conviction today).

God gave them His Spirit to sustain them through the trials of life. Paul said, *"Now it is God who makes both us and you stand firm in Christ. He anointed us, set his seal of ownership on us, and put his Spirit in our hearts as a deposit, guaranteeing what is to come"* (2 Cor. 1:21-22). Because of the baptism in the Holy Spirit, believers knew that God's presence was with them, sustaining them daily. They moved from victims to victors and relied on the Holy Spirit to lead, guide and direct them into all truth. Because of their faith and refusal to concede to the forces of evil, God gave them strength, wisdom, knowledge and understanding to witness for Jesus in Jerusalem, Judea, Samaria and to the ends of the earth.

Summary

The believers of the first century were powerless before they received the baptism in the Holy Spirit; but after He came, they were empowered to live out the faith. The church today needs to be renewed by the baptism in the Holy Spirit. Many believers love the Lord, but they do not have the boldness to witness for Christ, nor do they have the power to stand for righteousness. We, as believers, cannot compromise the Gospel of Jesus Christ. If the church will return to the biblical principles of engaging in fervent prayer, Bible study, praise and worship and eagerly desire the baptism, God will send His Spirit to baptize every regenerated Christian and empower us for service.

The baptism in the Holy Spirit enabled God's

people to proclaim the Gospel message throughout Asia Minor, Africa and Europe. Churches were planted and believers came together as a community of faith to worship God. They also gathered for preaching and teaching the Word of God. From the beginning, the church ministered to the spiritual, physical, emotional and economic needs of the people. As a result, the people witnessed the gifts in operation by the power of the Holy Spirit. The blind received sight; the lame walked; the dead were raised to life; the mute spoke again; and hearing was restored to the deaf. The Holy Spirit ministered healing in every area of their lives. Why was the church blessed so miraculously? It was because they turned their hearts to God. They decided that there was nothing that they wanted more than an intimate relationship with Jesus Christ and to declare His glory all over the world. Today's church needs that missionary zeal to evangelize the world.

The Holy Spirit is waiting to baptize believers and equip us for ministry, but the people must pray for the baptism. The baptism in the Holy Spirit is for empowerment. The enemy wants to deceive us and make us afraid to receive this great gift of God. Do not listen to him. Believe the Word of God; and read the testimony of the saints in Acts whose lives were changed because of the presence, power and indwelling of the Holy Spirit.

The church needs to be renewed so that it can take its rightful place of leadership in the world today.

PRAYER

(SURRENDER)

Almighty God,

I confess that I have sinned before You, and I am sorry. Please forgive me. I want to live holy so that I will be filled with the power of the Holy Spirit daily. I surrender my life to You, sacred, righteous Father, and I take comfort in Your Word, for You said that if I confess my sins, You are faithful and just and will forgive my sins and purify me from all unrighteousness. Hallelujah! I thank You, Almighty God, for my new beginning in You. In Jesus' name I pray. Amen. (1 John 1:9)

The next chapter will focus on selected renewal movements in church history that have rescued the church from spiritual stagnation and reaffirmed a commitment to follow God through the ministry of the Holy Spirit.

CHAPTER 4

THE RENEWAL OF THE CHURCH

"Create in me a pure heart, O God,
and renew a steadfast spirit within me"
(Ps. 51:10).

The church is a living body and must be continually renewed to prevent stagnation or decline. Many mainline denominations in the western world have lost their spiritual fervor, and their membership have suffered decline. C. Peter Wagner asserts:

> In the ten-year period from 1965 to 1975 the Episcopal Church lost 17 percent of its membership or 575,000 persons. The United Presbyterians lost 12 percent or 375,000 members. The United Methodists lost 10 percent or 1,100,000 members, and so on (Wagner 31-32).

Lyle E. Schaller reported a continuous decline in the inclusive membership of the above-mentioned denominations:

> In the twenty-six year period from 1968 to 1994 the Episcopal Church Membership declined from 3,373,890 to 2,504,682. The Presbyterian Church (U.S.A.) declined from 4,184,430 to 3,698,136. The United Methodist church declined from 10,990,720 to 8,584,125 (Schaller 124-125).

More recently, George Barna reported in 2001 that America is spiritually stagnant. According to Barna, there was:

> a small increase in the percentage of adults who can be classified as "born again" Christians (based upon their beliefs, not self-identification as "born again"), rising from 35% in 1991 to 41% in 2001. The four behaviors that declined in frequency – each measured in terms of participation in the previous week – were Bible reading (down from 45% to 37%); church attendance (down from 49% to 42%); volunteering at church (down from 27% to 20%); and adult Sunday school attendance (down from 23% to 19%) (Barna 1).

The church can reverse the downward spiral of stagnation and be renewed again, as it has done many times in the past, if we humble ourselves before God, reverently cry out to God for forgiveness of our sins, and make a decision to live for Christ alone.

Scriptural references for renewal theology are found in both the Old Testament and the New Testament. The Hebrew translation of the word "renew" in the Old Testament is *hadas*. It means "to make new, to give again" (Ps. 103:5; 104:30; Lam. 5:21). The Greek translation in the New Testament is *anakainoo*. It means "to make new" *(ana,* back or again*, kainos,* new) (Eph. 4:23). It also means "to grow up, revive, spring up, give new life'; *anakainosis* means "renewal" (Titus 3:5), "renewing power." (Bromiley 134 -135)

Scripture reveals that renewal brings new life. When people are renewed, they have a greater love for God and for one another. They have zeal to read and study God's Word, and their prayer life intensifies. Moreover, they seek to live a sanctified life, to serve in the church, to evangelize for Christ, to promote social reform, and to help improve the quality of life for others. Genuine renewal always results in a closer relationship with the Lord Jesus Christ and a passion for ministry. A glimpse at several renewal movements in church history on the following pages will provide a historical context for church renewal, from The Protestant Reformation in the sixteenth century to the Wesley Methodist Renewal Movement in the eighteenth century, to the Holiness Renewal Movement in the nineteenth century and to the Pentecostal and Charismatic Renewal Movement in the twentieth century.

The intent is not to present a comprehensive historical study of renewal of the church or a detailed analysis of the renewal movements; rather, the intent is to gain insight into how renewal patterns of the past have revived the church and how these renewal patterns can be instructive for the church today.

The Protestant Reformation

The Protestant Reformation in the sixteenth century was one of the greatest renewal movements in church history. This movement was started in response to the widespread abuse within the Roman Catholic Church. "The church systems of the late medieval era were notoriously corrupt, while its theology – rather like the academic theology of our own day – did nothing for religion either at the popular level or among the more educated of the time. (Babcock 87). The fundamental theology of the Reformers was a return to the Scriptures and the sacraments.

> The Protestant reformers were accused of being innovators, but they did not see themselves that way. Instead, they claimed to have rediscovered the ancient Pauline teaching that God's forgiveness is a free gift bestowed without consideration of human merit. This renewed emphasis on faith alone in God's grace alone, combined with their views on the Bible, Church, sacraments, and priesthood, gave the different forms of Protestant Christianity their distinctive identities (Nystrom and Nystrom 225).

The two larger branches of the Protestant Reformation were the Magisterial Reformers and the Radical Reformers. "Luther, Zwingli and Calvin led what is sometimes called the Magisterial Reformation, so named because it used the civil authority of the magistrates to further its agenda" (Saint-Claire 7). The Anabaptists were the leaders of the Radical Reformers and they were greatly persecuted by the Roman Catholic Church and the Magisterial Reformers, primarily because they did not believe in infant baptism.

Martin Luther

Martin Luther, a Roman Catholic monk, was the first and best known of the Magisterial Reformers. Luther was tormented by his sins and agonized over how a holy God could accept him. Luther disagreed with the Roman Catholic Church on many theological viewpoints, chief among which was the selling of indulgences. "In Roman Catholicism, (indulgences provided) remission of the temporal, especially purgatorial, consequences of previously forgiven sins" (Erickson 83). Luther rejected this church doctrine because he could not find scriptural support for it; and the doctrine did not provide him with the internal peace that he so desperately needed. Luther prayed to God, and he studied the Scriptures assiduously seeking insight to God's holy Word that would bring resolution to the tension in his life. God answered Luther's prayers through the reading of the Book of Romans, and his life was transformed:

Deeply troubled in conscience and aware from Scripture of the depth of his sin, he wrestled with the words of Romans 1:17, 'The righteous will live by faith.' That statement, itself a quote from Habakkuk in the Old Testament, convinced Luther that 'through grace and sheer mercy God justifies us through faith.' Salvation is not by our good works or any other merit of ourselves, our church, or our religion: It is through Jesus Christ alone (Elwell and Yarbrough 275).

Luther was instantly delivered from the guilt and self-condemnation he had suffered for so long, and he did not remain quiet about his feelings. "At noon on October 31, 1517, he posted on the door of the Castle Church in Wittenberg his 'Ninety-five Theses or Disputations on the Power and Efficacy of Indulgences.' This action was terribly ordinary. The door was the bulletin board for the university, and like other such notices, Luther's included an invitation to public discussion" (Nystrom 231). Although no one responded to his invitation, this courageous act sparked the beginning of the Protestant Reformation in Germany. Luther expounded the theology of justification by faith, the authority of Scripture, and the priesthood of all believers.

His position was briefly that the Roman Catholic Church and the papacy have no divine right in things spiritual; that the Scripture, not the priest or the church, has final authority over conscience. 'Whatever is not against Scripture is for Scripture, and Scripture is for it,' said Luther. People are forgiven and absolved of their sins, he believed, not by good works or by imposition of church rite – and especially not through the purchase of indulgences offered for sale by the Roman Catholic Church – but by their Holy Spirit-empowered action in turning from sin directly to God (Mead 142).

Luther never intended to leave the church; rather, his intent was to work within the church structure to share his newfound revelation of God's Word and to ignite the flame of renewal and reform within the church. Unfortunately, the Roman Catholic Church did not endorse his theology, and he was eventually excommunicated. This action led to the founding of the Lutheran denomination that was based on Martin Luther's theology. The church placed a strong emphasis on salvation through grace alone (*sola gratia*), by faith alone (*sola fide*), which meant that the selling of indulgences by the church was unbiblical. Lutherans believed the Word of God was central to the faith and saw the role of the Spirit "as making effective and living in the church God's forgiveness of sins in Christ, which comes not through the law but through grace, and which the preaching of the word is constantly to hold before the church as that which is to guide the whole of the church's life and witness in and to the world" (Barr and Yocum 97- 98). In time, this movement spread from Germany to the Scandinavian countries, Greenland, North America, South America, Africa and India.

Ulrich Zwingli

Parallel to this movement was the work of Ulrich Zwingli, the leader of the Reformation in Zurich in 1520. Like Luther, Zwingli believed that the Bible and not the church was the sole authority (*sola scriptura*) for Christians; however, he disagreed with Luther on the theology of the Sacrament of Holy Communion. Luther believed in consubstantiation, which is "the idea, characteristic of Lutheran theology, that in the Lord's Supper the bread and wine are not transformed into the body and blood of Christ, but that the molecules of the flesh and blood are present 'in, with, and under' the molecules of the bread and wine" (Erickson 36). "Zwingli rejected such a notion. For him, the Eucharist was a mere memorial of Jesus' death, a ritual sign Jesus left his church by which to remember his act of self-surrender. The bread and wine of the Eucharist did not change in their being; at best, they changed in their significance because of the context in which they were received" (Saint-Clair 4).

John Calvin

John Calvin was a second-generation reformer after Luther and Zwingli. The reformation was not looked upon favorably in his native country of France, so he fled to Geneva in 1536 to continue his work. Calvin's theology was expounded in his Institutes of the Christian Religion, which became the Reformed tradition's most complete and systematic statement of faith. Like Luther, he saw a need for the church to return to Scripture, and the only way Scripture could be understood was by the Holy Spirit. "Scripture is considered basic and normative, but its guidance can only be rightly heard and obeyed through the *testimonium spiritus sancti internum,* the inner witness of the Holy Spirit. And this is said to be as true for the church as a whole as it is for individual believers" (Barr and Yocum 99). Like Luther and Zwingli, Calvin endorsed the Sacrament of Baptism of Infants; however, his view differed from both Luther and Zwingli on the theology of the Sacrament of Holy Communion (he called it the Lord's Supper). Calvin believed in *"Dynamic presence,"* which is "a reference to the view that the body and blood of Christ are present in the Lord's Supper not literally and physically, but spiritually and influentially" (Erickson 46). His work led to the formation of the Reformed Tradition and gave birth to the Presbyterian Church. The movement spread from Geneva to Scotland and North America.

The Anabaptists

The Radical Reformation began in Zurich in the early 1520s. Unlike the Magisterial Reformers, they believed in the separation of church and state and rejected the assistance of the magistrates as well as the teachings of the Magisterial Reformers that they felt were not substantiated in Scripture. The Anabaptists, led by Conrad Grebel, discredited Zwingli's work, because, in their opinion, Zwingli did not do enough to reform the church, and he continued to accept the assistance of the state. However, perhaps the primary area of disagreement between The Magisterial Reformers and The Radical Reformers was the sacrament of infant baptism. The Magisterial Reformers sanctioned infant baptism, while The Radical Reformers rejected infant baptism and endorsed the sacrament of believer baptism only. They believed so strongly in this point of view that they defied the Roman Catholic Church and the Magisterial Reformers by their refusal to baptize infants. Moreover, they rebaptized all of their followers who had been baptized as infants. This angered Zwingli so much that he called them Anabaptists ("rebaptizers"). Many Anabaptists refused to recant their beliefs and suffered martyrdom through burning at the stake, drowning, and other horrific methods inflicted upon them by "the church." However, the movement survived, and several denominations trace their history back to The Radical Reformation, including the Mennonites and Swiss Brethren.

The Magisterial and Radical branches of the Reformation were formed to bring renewal and restoration to the Church. Unfortunately, they allowed theological and ecclesiological concerns to separate them. Nevertheless, despite the differences and divisions within Reformation theology, Protestantism continued to spread throughout Europe, North America, South America and Africa, and many denominations were birthed through these renewal movements.

The English Reformation

The Reformation continued to spread throughout the world, and the English Reformation began in 1534. England separated from the Roman Catholic Church because King Henry VIII wanted the church to grant his divorce to his wife Catherine of Aragon, since she had not produced a male heir. The Roman Catholic Church's refusal to do so angered Henry; consequently, he found support among other theologians and university faculties. "The king followed a course of expediency; he married Anne Boleyn in 1533, and two months later he had the archbishop of Canterbury pronounce his divorce from Catherine. Henry was then excommunicated by the pope, but retaliated in 1534 by having Parliament pass an act appointing the king and his successors supreme head of the Church of England, thus establishing an independent national Anglican church. Further legislation cut off the pope's English revenues and ended his political and religious authority in England (Encarta Encyclopedia 8). Classical Anglican theology included the Book of Common Prayer, which was written in English, and Thirty Nine Articles of Religion.

The Methodist Renewal Movement

As the church entered the eighteenth century, there was a need for renewal again. The major branches of the Reformation (Lutheranism, Reformed, and Anglicanism) became stagnant. Most of the denominations lost their spiritual fervor and no longer had a passion for the Word of God. In fact, the church entered a period of scholasticism, which was "the type of theology practiced by Protestantism and particularly by Lutheranism in the seventeenth century. It was concerned primarily with defining correct doctrine through a series of subtle arguments" (Erickson 148).

People attended church, but worship was cold and rote. Many were there out of habit, tradition and responsibility, but they were not concerned about spiritual growth. They were spiritually dead. Garth Rosell, church historian, suggests that one could write "Ichabod" (the glory has departed) on their services. Rosell contends that when spiritual depravity occurs, the church looks alive; people are still functioning and going about their duties, but they have lost their spiritual fervor and left their first love, Jesus Christ (Rosell Audio 5). The prophet Eli's daughter-in-law named her newborn son Ichabod, as she lay dying in childbirth. Scripture records,

> *His daughter-in-law, the wife of Phinehas, was pregnant and near the time of delivery. When she heard the news that the ark of God had been captured and that her father-in-law and her husband were dead, she went into labor and gave birth, but was overcome by her labor pains. As she was dying, the women attending her said, "Don't despair: you have given birth to a son." But she did not respond or pay attention. She named the boy Ichabod, saying, "The*

*glory has departed from Israel" – because of
the capture of the ark of God and the deaths of
her father-in-law and her husband. She said,
"The glory has departed from Israel, for the ark
of God has been captured." (1 Sam. 4:19-22)*

Many denominations are faced with that challenge today. Will the people continue to attend service week after week without experiencing a new level of spirituality? Can they be content just going to the house of worship, but not giving themselves fully to the worship of God? Political and social compromises have caused the church to experience a spiritual drought, and there is a spiritual famine in the land; but the church does not have to die; it can be renewed! It is God's will to see His people praise Him and worship Him in spirit and in truth as we serve Him faithfully and witness to the Gospel of Jesus Christ. We can prevent "Ichabod" from being written on the doors of the sanctuary and the lives of the people if we walk by the Holy Spirit and not buy into cultural trends that violate God's holy Word.

As the eighteenth century progressed, the Anglican Church experienced spiritual decline. There was a lack of piety among the people; many of the priests and parishioners alike were no longer committed to living holy and reverently before God. Yet a remnant of God's people was praying for renewal. God, in His infinite mercy, answered their prayers and called the Wesley family for service. Suzette Wesley was a strong Christian woman who loved God deeply; and she taught her children to love and honor God in all of their ways. She felt that God had a special call on her son, John, after he was saved from the fire in their home. John agreed with his mother that God had indeed called him into the service of the Lord, and he had a passion for holiness, righteousness and purity. John and his brother Charles, were gifted, loved the Anglican Church and desired to see it renewed. Their desire was to reach the disenfranchised and the poor who were neglected by the church.

John and Charles entered the priesthood and enrolled at Oxford University. Along with some of their friends, John and Charles made a commitment to live holy and to come together at the same time every morning for daily devotions, worship, prayer and Bible study. Other students began to ridicule them and gave them the name "Methodists" because they were so methodical and disciplined. They were referred to as members of the "Holy Club." Both of these terms, "Methodists" and "Holy Club," were meant to be derogatory, but the Wesleys and their colleagues did not allow anyone to deter them from their dedication to the Lord. They were determined to live for God and to disregard the criticism and ridicule of their classmates. These brothers served God based on their spiritual gifts. Charles' love for God was expressed primarily through his gift of music. He wrote and composed hundreds of hymns, many of which we still sing today. John's love for God was expressed through his gift of leadership.

John had a passion for missions and traveled to Georgia (in America) as a missionary in 1738 before he was converted. Consequently, his missionary journey was a failure; nevertheless, he continued to seek God. On the ship back to England, John met and was influenced by a group of Moravians. After his return to England, he attended a Moravian Brethren meeting on Alders Gate Street in London on May 24, 1738, which transformed his life. As the leader read from Luther's preface to his Romans commentary, John was converted. He described the experience:

> "While he was describing the change which God works in the heart through faith in Christ, I felt my heart strangely warmed. I felt that I did trust in Christ, Christ alone for my salvation: And an assurance was given me, that he had taken away my sins, even mine, and saved me from the law of sin and death" (Elwell 275).

After John's conversion, his commitment to Christ increased. He continued his duties as an Anglican priest within the confines of the church, and he also evangelized outside of the church. John preached in the fields or wherever the people were. He felt an urgency to proclaim the Gospel so that all who heard could be saved. Scholars have credited him with coining the phrase "a personal relationship with Jesus Christ." Although he never left the Anglican Church, John spearheaded renewal from within. His quest for holiness spawned the beginning of the Methodist Church in 1739. He was called the Father of Methodism. John Wesley introduced the theology of the "Double Cure." He believed that there are two separate and distinct acts of grace in the Christian experience: Salvation (justification by faith in Jesus Christ) and Sanctification. Salvation is the first act of grace that is received at conversion, but then a second crisis experience, a second act of grace, is needed to live out the faith, which he called sanctification, or perfect love. The two acts of grace represent the Double Cure. His views were expounded fully in his tract, <u>A Plan Account of Christian Perfection (1776).</u>

The goals of Methodism are to improve the spiritual life of the church and to take care of the sick and needy. The primary tenets are:

- The Bible as the ultimate authority.
- God's universal love for all persons.
- Justification by faith in Jesus Christ.
- Sanctification as the pursuit of scriptural holiness.
- The assurance of salvation that comes through the Holy Spirit.
- Christian perfection achieved through personal holiness and social justice (American Bible Society 2).

The Methodist denomination was the first great holiness church. They loved to sing and praise God and were uninhibited in their worship of God. Methodism spread all over the world and was established in America at the historic Christmas Conference in Baltimore, Maryland, in 1784. Richard

Allen, a former slave and Methodist minister, was one of two persons of African descent present at the Christmas Conference.

Several American denominations trace their lineage to the Methodist Church. They include The African Methodist Episcopal Church (1787); The African Methodist Episcopal Zion Church (1796); The Free Methodist Church (1860); The Christian Methodist Episcopal Church (1870); and The United Methodist Church (1968).

The African Methodist Episcopal Church

The African Methodist Episcopal Church, unlike other religious groups, did not have its origin in a theological or doctrinal dispute. The Church was founded as a protest against racial discrimination. Richard Allen, the founder and first Bishop of the Church, was born into slavery on February 14, 1760, in Philadelphia, Pennsylvania. At the age of 17, he was converted at a Methodist meeting. Allen had a great desire to proclaim the Gospel of Jesus Christ, and in 1782, he was licensed to preach. After buying his freedom for $2,000, he became an itinerant preacher. In 1786, Richard Allen returned to Philadelphia and joined St. George's Methodist Episcopal Church, where he served on the ministerial staff. His preaching inspired persons of all races to join St. George's and the church experienced rapid growth. Initially, the races worshipped together in harmony; however, as the parishioners of African descent increased, the Caucasian parishioners began to discriminate against them and wanted to relegate them to a segregated section of the church. The Caucasian believers ceased to enjoy the unity of believers worshipping God together in spirit and in truth.

In 1787, the discrimination against parishioners of African descent escalated. Howard Gregg recounts the event that led to the founding of the African Methodist Episcopal Church:

The immediate cause of the organization of the A.M.E. Church was the fact that members of St. George's Methodist Episcopal Church in Philadelphia, PA, in the year 1787 segregated its colored members from its white communicants. The Blacks were sent to the gallery of the church, to use the venerable Richard Allen's own words. One Sunday as these Africans, as they were called, knelt to pray outside of their segregated area they were actually pulled from their knees and told to go to a place which had been designated for them. This, of course, was adding insult to injury, and the Negroes said, 'Wait until prayer is over and we will go out and trouble you no more.' The Negroes went out and formed the Free African Society, and from this Society came two groups: The Episcopalians and the Methodists. The leader of the Methodist group was Richard Allen, the African Preacher. This was a revolt against segregation, and from the beginning, anyone except a slaveholder, could join the newly- formed church (Gregg 12-13).

The Free African Society sparked the flame of spiritual renewal and social reform among African-Americans. Its purpose was:

> To preserve the worship experience that brought persons of color together in spiritual fellowship. It was instrumental in looking out for the sick, in providing for the poor and unemployed, and in the promotion of high moral standards and better cooperation among the races. It advocated self-help and self-development (Foster 30).

Richard Allen and his wife Sarah Allen were concerned about the whole person. In addition to spiritual growth, they wanted the people to receive an education. Many of the parishioners were former slaves who had been denied the right to an education, so Allen started night classes in their home and taught the people how to read and to write. Sarah Allen became the first missionary of the Church. Moreover, Richard Allen and Absalom Jones founded the first insurance company by African-Americans in Philadelphia. It was called The Mutual Aide Society. Its purpose was to provide protection and care for widows and orphans of deceased members.

Allen used his own resources to purchase a blacksmith shop, which they used for worship. In 1794, Bishop Francis Asbury of the Methodist Church dedicated the first African Methodist Episcopal Church, Bethel Methodist Episcopal Church, located at Sixth Street and Lombard in Philadelphia, Pennsylvania. (The church is still there today). In 1799, Allen was ordained a deacon by Bishop Asbury and became the pastor of Bethel. Allen convened the first "General Convention" in Philadelphia, Pennsylvania, April 9-11, 1816. He called together the leadership of other African-American churches, which were fighting for their independence from Caucasian leadership. Those present represented churches from Baltimore, Maryland; Salem, New Jersey; Attleboro, Pennsylvania; and Wilmington, Delaware. The conference passed a resolution to form the African Methodist Episcopal Church, and Richard Allen served as the first African-American Bishop. Jarena Lee was the first female preacher in the African Methodist Episcopal Church in the nineteenth century, and Rev. Dr. Vashti McKenzie became the first woman Bishop in the African Methodist Episcopal Church in 2000.

Each word in the name of the church has a significant meaning:

- African - acknowledges that people of African descent founded the church; however, the church does not discriminate. Membership is open to all people.
- Methodist – the Church's lineage is traced back to the Methodist Church. The polity of the church is based on Methodism.
- Episcopal - refers to the structure of the A.M.E. Church. Bishops govern churches in Episcopal Districts.

The A.M.E. Church has been a bedrock for the African-American community since its inception and today has a membership of over 3,000,000 people in more than 4,000 churches. The churches are located in nineteen Episcopal Districts throughout North America, South America, Africa, Europe and the Caribbean. Each District is constructed to facilitate the supervision of the activities of the churches under the leadership of a Presiding Bishop. I was blessed to serve under the leadership of Bishop John R. Bryant and Rev. Dr. Cecelia Williams Bryant in the Tenth Episcopal District during their tenure (1990-2000). The A.M.E. Church oversees eleven colleges and four seminaries in the United States and Africa.

The Holiness Renewal Movement

In the nineteenth century the Methodist Church strayed away from the holiness teachings of John Wesley and drifted into modernist/liberal theology. The older members of the church were very dissatisfied and wanted the church to be renewed. The familiar method they chose to re-kindle their spiritual fervor was Camp Meetings. The National Holiness Camp Association was begun in Vineland, New Jersey, in 1867. The services were attended by as many as 20,000 who had a burning desire to return to the teachings of John Wesley and live out the faith.

In 1875, the meaning of Wesley's "second blessing – sanctification" theology was expanded. The American holiness movement placed emphasis on the Pentecostal aspects and now called the second blessing of sanctification "Pentecostal sanctification." Vinson Synan contends, "practically all the hymns of the early Pentecostal movement were produced by holiness writers celebrating the second blessing as both a cleansing and an enduement of power" (Synan 3). The Camp Meetings were at the heart of the Wesleyan/holiness renewal movement. Thousands testified to receiving the baptism in the Holy Spirit. This movement grew tremendously from 1867 to 1880. Rossell asserts,

> By 1880 there were 67 National Camp Meetings; 28 campgrounds; 206 holiness evangelists; 354 weekly holiness meetings in private homes and 41 holiness periodicals being published. The deep yearning of the holiness movement was to return to the old Wesleyan vision and do so in these summer conferences (Rosell Audio 5).

According to Barbara J. Machaffie, Women were active in the preaching ministry of the church:

> Luther Lee, the founder of the Wesleyan Methodist Church, reflected the thinking of John Wesley in his belief that women had a right to preach the gospel. He preached the sermon at the ordination of Antoinette Brown, pointing to female prophets in the Old Testament and women 'ministers' in the New. Later in the century, the Methodist evangelist W. B.

Godbey could write, 'It is a God-given, blood-bought privilege, and bounden duty of the women as well as the men, to preach the gospel.' The large Methodist Episcopal Church issued local preaching licenses to women until 1880 (Machaffie 109).

MacHaffie contends that Phoebe Palmer was one of the great leaders of the holiness movement. "Phoebe Palmer was a major force behind the movement. She traveled as an evangelist throughout the United States, Great Britain, and Canada, and it was under her influence that Catherine Booth and Frances Willard were called to public ministry. Booth did as much as her husband, William, to establish the Salvation Army. She was an outstanding revival preacher who believed firmly in the equality of women with men in all spheres" (Ibid 109).

Amanda Berry Smith, an African American woman, was another great holiness preacher. Ms. Smith faced both racism and sexism in her plight to proclaim the Gospel of Jesus Christ, but she refused to succumb to either of the evils. God used her to preach in the United States, England, India and West Africa.

The holiness movement was accepted in churches until it met resistance from the liberals in 1880. Eventually, those involved in the holiness movement realized they could not renew the church from within. They were not drawing the churches back from liberalism to the old Wesleyan theology of living out the faith in holiness. From the 1880s to the 1890s the members of the Wesleyan/holiness Methodist movement felt it was necessary to separate from the liberal churches. This group was known as the "come-outers." During this period, the "come-outers" formed 23 separate denominations that were based on Wesleyan/holiness theology. These included the Church of God in Christ (1897) and the Pentecostal Holiness Church (1898). They retained the Wesleyan double cure (justification and sanctification) and added a triple cure, the baptism in the Holy Spirit as the third blessing (Rosell Audiotape 5).

The Pentecostal and Charismatic Renewal Movements

In the early twentieth century renewal came to the church through the Pentecostal movement. Frank S. Mead defines Pentecostalism as "an inclusive term applied to a large number of revivalistic American sects, assemblies, and churches. Many have either a Methodist or Baptist background, and they are primarily concerned with perfection, holiness and the Pentecostal experience....The churches do not always include the word Pentecostal in their name" (Synan 2). This movement was born out of the soil of the Holiness Movement, which traced its heritage back to Methodism and the teachings of John Wesley "It was Wesley's colleague, John Fletcher, however, who first called this second blessing a 'baptism in the Holy Spirit,' an experience which brought spiritual power to the recipient as well as inner cleansing" (Synan 2).

Modern Pentecostalism began in association with the teaching and preaching of Rev. Charles Parham at the Bethel Bible School in 1900, but Rev. William Joseph Seymour, an African American minister, is credited as the father of Modern Pentecostalism, because the movement did not receive worldwide acclaim until Rev. Seymour birthed the Azuza Street Revival meetings in Los Angeles, California, in 1906.

Charles Parham was a Methodist minister of the "come-outer" group. He lived in Topeka, Kansas, but had been greatly influenced by the Fire Baptized Holiness Church of Iowa. This church endorsed the Wesleyan double cure theology but added a third experience of grace, "the fire of the baptism in the Holy Spirit," which they called the "triple cure." Parham opened Bethel Bible School in Topeka with 40 students. They began their quest for spiritual gifts by studying the Book of Acts.

On New Year's Eve at the turn of the century (1901), they were all together praying. The class laid hands on one of the students, Agnes Ozman, and she began to speak in tongues. Up until this time, spiritual gifts had been dormant in this country for a very long time. Parham and the other students also spoke in tongues, and Parham posited the belief that speaking in tongues was the initial evidence of receiving the baptism in the Holy Spirit. This viewpoint is still debated among Christians today.

In 1905, Charles Parham traveled to Houston, Texas, where he opened a Bible school with 25 students. One of his students was Rev. William Joseph

Seymour (W.J. Seymour) from Louisiana. Seymour was an African American pastor who came to study with Parham because he had heard about the triple cure, but he was not treated with the dignity and respect of other students. According to Cheryl J. Sanders:

> When Seymour enrolled in Parham's classes in Houston, he was subjected to the indignity of having to sit in a hall where he could hear the classes through the doorway, in keeping with the Southern system of racial segregation. Seymour accepted Parham's advocacy of tongues-speaking, but rejected his racist prejudices and polemics (Sanders 28).

While studying in Houston, Seymour met Neely Terry and accepted her invitation to pastor a Nazarene church in Los Angeles, where she was a member. The text of Seymour's first sermon was Acts 2:4: *"and they were all filled with the Holy Ghost, and began to speak in tongues, as the Spirit gave them utterance" (KJV).* Lawrence Neale Jones recounts,

> His first sermon was the last sermon he was to preach at this Nazarene congregation, for most of its members found his doctrinal stance offensive. Subsequently, Seymour was befriended by a Mr. & Mrs. Asbury, who were members of the church, and he began to hold services in their home. On April 9, 1906, the Holy Spirit bap-

tized seven seekers and they began to speak in tongues. So great was the impact of their experience that the meeting continued uninterruptedly for three days (Jones 146).

The revival grew so rapidly that Seymour and his followers had to find a larger place to accommodate the people. They moved to a former African Methodist Episcopal Church building located at 312 Azusa Street in the heart of Los Angeles. People came from all over the world to witness this revival and to receive the baptism in the Holy Spirit at the Apostolic Faith Mission, pastored by Rev. W.J. Seymour. For over three years the Apostolic Faith Mission had services three times a day, seven days a week. It was reported that thousands of people received the baptism in the Holy Spirit and took the teaching and vision back to their home churches, where they proclaimed the power of the Holy Spirit and brought renewal to their respective churches.

Those who participated in the Azusa Street Revival were ridiculed and mocked by the media. *The Los Angeles Times* of April 18, 1906 reported "weird babbles of tongues, new sect of fanatics breaking loose on Azusa Street" (Sanders 29). Seymour was not discouraged by the criticism of the press. He founded *The Apostolic Faith Paper* and sent out 50,000 copies to subscribers, free of charge. The flame of renewal spread from Azusa Street in Los Angeles, California, to the uttermost parts of the world.

Oftentimes, when there is a great move of the

Holy Spirit, people will misunderstand and make accusations against believers. Pioneering Christians frequently encountered hostility and opposition; nevertheless, they persevered in the strong name of Jesus Christ and the power of the Holy Spirit. The New Testament witness for this type of ridicule is found on the day of Pentecost. After the believers were baptized in the Holy Spirit, onlookers accused them of being drunk. Peter and the eleven stood up and declared that they were not drunk; and Peter used that opportunity to proclaim the Good News of the Gospel of Jesus Christ. He declared, *"Men of Israel, listen to this: Jesus of Nazareth was a man accredited by God to you by miracles, wonders and signs, which God did among you through him, as you yourselves know. This man was handed over to you by God's set purpose and foreknowledge; and you, with the help of wicked men, put Him to death by nailing him to the cross. But God raised him from the dead, freeing him from the agony of death, because it was impossible for death to keep its hold on him"* (Acts 2:23-24). Peter told them if they would repent and be baptized, they would *"receive the gift of the Holy Spirit. The promise is for you and your children and for all who are far off – for all whom the Lord our God will call"* (Acts 2:38-39). The Holy Spirit convicted the hearers of the message and *"Those who accepted his message were baptized, and about three thousand were added to their number that day"* (Acts 2:41). No one can stop the move of the Holy Spirit!

Women were very active in the Azusa Street

Revival (in fact, Rev. Seymour's wife became the pastor of the church after her husband's death); and the Revival was mixed racially from the very beginning, in contrast to the other Protestant churches in America in 1906. Elder C. H. Mason of the Church of God in Christ in Arkansas attended the revival in 1907 and received the baptism in the Holy Spirit. When he returned to Arkansas, he ordained many white ministers who needed ministerial credentials to carry out their duties. However, the unity of believers was soon to be divided along racial lines. In 1914, some white ministers met in Hot Springs, Arkansas, and formed the Assembly of God denomination. Michael Hamilton contends:

> With the founding of the Assembly of God it became clear that Pentecostals moved toward institutionalizing the movement that would follow the prevailing cultural practice of segregating the race structurally. Thus, a movement, which began in a shared religious experience and which was rooted in a theological consensus succumbed early to the acids of racist thinking. However, it should be pointed out that even today several of the predominately white Pentecostal bodies have Black members. (Hamilton149).

The Pentecostal movement experienced renewal through the baptism in the Holy Spirit and the use of *charisms*, "spiritual gifts." While many mainline Protestant denominations are in decline, this renewal movement experienced tremendous growth in the twentieth century. Synan records the statistical data on the Pentecostal and Charismatic movements, which he said could best be described in three waves:

> The first wave produced the Classical Pentecostal Movement, an outgrowth of the Azusa Street Revival with Rev. William Joseph Seymour in 1906. This movement gave birth to 11,000 Pentecostal denominations worldwide. The second wave was the Neo-Pentecostal movement and the Charismatic Renewal movement. The Neo-Pentecostal movement started in the Episcopal, Presbyterian and Baptist denominations. These denominations began to find groups of parishioners in their churches who embraced the Pentecostal/Charismatic movement. Scholars believe that Dennis Bennett, Rector of St. Mark's Episcopal Church in Van Nuys, California, began this renewal movement in 1960. Within a decade, this movement had spread to all the 150 major Protestant families of the world reaching a total of 55,000,000 people by 1990. God's Spirit brought renewal to His church across denominational lines. The Roman Catholic Church Charismatic Renewal movement began in 1967 at Duquesne University and Notre Dame University.

> In the 26 years since its inception, the Catholic movement has touched the lives of over

70,000,000 Catholics in over 120 nations of the world. The third wave is the fusing together of the Charismatic within the main-line denominations so that it is no longer on the fringes, nor can it be distinguished or considered a separate entity. This movement originated at Fuller Theological Seminary in 1981 under the classroom ministry of John Wimber. This movement consisted of mainline Evangelicals who moved in signs and wonders, but who disdained labels such as Pentecostal or Charismatic. By 1990 this group numbered some 33,000,000 members in the world (Synan 9 – paraphrased).

Summary

The renewal movements from the Protestant Reformation to the Pentecostal and Charismatic Renewal Movements spanned 483 years. During this time, the Church has experienced seasons of spiritual and numerical growth followed too often by seasons of decline. Therefore, it is crucial that believers seek to live godly lives and pray for the Holy Spirit to bring seasons of refreshing and renewal through the baptism in the Holy Spirit. This gift is available to every regenerated Christian. God is not a respecter of persons, nor is He a denominational God. His presence and His power are available to all born-again Christians.

Throughout church history, ordinary people have fulfilled extraordinary missions for God as they willingly submitted to the leading of the Holy Spirit. Many of the leaders of the renewal movements did not use the term, "baptized in the Holy Spirit," but clearly it was His presence that brought renewal to the church and transformed the lives of the people. Dr. Delbert Vaughn, founder of The Houston Graduate School of Theology, states correctly,

> One thing that we learn from studying the history of the ways and means of the Spirit is that He may not come to people the same way in each period of the church life. But when the Holy Spirit does come upon His people, He always comes through truth, in peace and in purity. He always comes in ways that are in harmony with the Holy Scriptures. He comes in unity with the Father and the Son. He comes to unify His church in grace and love. He is not the author of confusion. He is the author of peace and of sound mind. As the just shall live and move and have their being by faith, so by faith the just shall be baptized with the powers of the Trinity and sanctified by the Holy Spirit (Vaughn 119-120).

If the church is to experience renewal today, we must learn from the renewal movements of the past and have the faith to trust the Holy Spirit to lead and guide us into all truth. Remember the great Protestant Reformation principle: The church once reformed must always be reforming itself so that it remains alive and on the cutting-edge of effective societal change.

It is time to put away denominational differences, to stop fighting over the *charisms* (spiritual gifts), and to seek God in prayer. Genuine renewal will come to the people of God when they humble themselves and realize that God's Spirit is superior to their tradition. The church must maintain its spiritual fervor and seek spiritual growth and maturity as it engages in spiritual warfare daily. Let the past guide the future. The renewal movements of the last 483 years provide clear evidence that when the people have a passion for God, God will interrupt traditions and breathe new life into His church. Genuine renewal will produce a deeper love for God and for one another. The people will desire to study and obey the Word of God, and they will have a zeal for true ministry.

Most mainline denominations need to be renewed. I believe it will come as the church yields to the leading of the Holy Spirit and refuses to compromise the Word of God.

PRAYER

(Sovereign)

Gracious Father,

I humble myself before You and I ask You to deliver me from every evil (sexism, racism, ungodly liberalism) that seeks to interfere with Your divine will. I acknowledge that You alone are sovereign, and I place my life in Your hands. My heart's desire is to forsake all else and follow You. I pray that Your will be done in my life and the life of Your Church now and forevermore, by the power of the Holy Spirit. In Jesus' name. Amen. (Matt. 26:42).

In the next chapter I will report on the case study I conducted for my doctoral project on renewal of the church through the baptism in the Holy Spirit and spiritual gifts.

CHAPTER 5

THE CASE STUDY ON THE BAPTISM IN THE HOLY SPIRIT AND SPIRITUAL GIFTS

""Study to shew thyself approved unto God, a workman that needeth not to be ashamed, rightly dividing the word of truth."
(2 Ti. 2:15 KJV)

So many churches have lost their spiritual fervor. Many people attend service out of habit. The responsive reading is rote and the order of service is predictable. Are they growing? Are they cultivating an intimate relationship with the Lord Jesus Christ? God wants His people to be excited about worship. He wants them to expect Him to move supernaturally in their services and in their lives daily. I believe that much of the dissatisfaction that parishioners feel stems from serving in the wrong area of ministry. They need to serve in areas in which they have been gifted. However, many parishioners do not know their spiritual gifts, nor do they realize how important it is to seek God's guidance before making a commitment to any area of service. I believe that a change will occur in the church when parishioners are given an opportunity to discover and use their spiritual gifts. Therefore, I conducted a case study that focused on the renewal of the church.

The ministry site for this project was Wayman Chapel African Methodist Episcopal Church in Houston, Texas, where Rev. M. C. Cooper served as pastor. The African Methodist Episcopal Church has a rich history of reliance on the power of the Holy Spirit in the ministry of the church. Bishop Henry McNeil Turner wrote:

> The speaker for God may lack all else that gives human lips audience, yet having this power he has that which qualifies him for the work, though it may be unseemly done by human estimates, may gain but shame to the speaker. Although endued with all aggregated forces which captivate, convince, and enforce truth or opinions in the judgment; yet if he lacks this power, which is not taught in earthly schools or imposed by human hands or learned by artful rules, which defies rhetoric, taste, eloquence, his ministry by God's estimate and in spiritual results will fall far below zero.

> God does not mix this power with other solutions to give it efficiency. It is not some or much of the Holy Ghost mixed with some or much of

other ingredients. This power is from the Holy Ghost singular and alone. It is the one thing to be sought and secured, the one thing whose importance discredits all other things, the one thing which stands alone unrivaled, super eminent. The circumstances and dignity of official position, the show of human learning, the vain adornments of a vicious eloquence must be despised in the pursuit of this absolutely essential,all-important one thing (Turner 272).

I developed an instructional program to lead students through a teaching on the basic tenets of the person and work of the Holy Spirit with special emphasis on the baptism in the Holy Spirit and the utilization of spiritual gifts. The objective was to demystify the ministry of the Holy Spirit and to ignite the flame of renewal in the church. I proceeded using a well-established five-step structure:

1. <u>Discovery stage</u>. Created a pre-test to assess the need for teaching on this subject matter (Appendix A).
2. <u>Planning and organizing stage</u>. Prepared a study that focused on the importance of the ministry of the Holy Spirit for church renewal.
3. <u>Implementation stage</u>. Conducted a six-week teaching session based on the course syllabus (Appendix B). A series of key passages on the baptism in the Holy Spirit in Acts 1:4-8; 2:1-4; 8:5-13; 10:44-48; 19:1-6 served as the intellectual model of the project, as well as

Scripture references on the gifts of the Holy Spirit in Romans 12:3-8; Ephesians 4:11; First Corinthians 12:4-11; 14:1-25. The text used to design the discovery of spiritual gifts section of the project was <u>Your Spiritual Gifts Can Help Your Church Grow</u> by C. Peter Wagner.

4. <u>Measurement stage</u>. Created and administered a post-test to all participants (Appendix C). This instrument was used to measure the effectiveness of the project.

5. <u>Evaluation stage</u>. Participants completed a course evaluation form (Appendix D). This instrument was used to evaluate the teaching and the course material.

<u>Demographics from the Pre-Test Questionnaire</u>

Participation in the study was open to all persons who wanted to experience renewal in their personal lives and in the life of the church. There were 24 participants. All of the participants had accepted Jesus Christ as their personal Lord and Savior. The participants were from different churches. Eighty-three percent were from the site church; thirteen percent were from other churches; and four percent did not list their local church affiliation (see Chart 1 located at the end of this section). The age categories of participants ranged from 20 to 80. The age group 41-50 represented the largest category at 38 percent (Chart 2). The gender distribution was 58 percent females and 42 percent males (Chart 3) and the majority of the participants, 71 percent, were married (Chart 4) I taught for 75 minutes each week, and at the end of the lecture, thirty minutes was reserved for discussion, comments, questions/answers, prayer requests, and closing prayers.

At the initial meeting, participants were given a pre-test questionnaire to complete (Appendix A). This pre-test was also used to assess each person's understanding of the ministry of the Holy Spirit and to adapt the course material accordingly.

Purpose and Goals of the Participants

The participants were asked why they chose to be a part of this study. Twenty-five percent responded that they wanted to become stronger in God's Word; twenty-five percent wanted to find out their spiritual gifts and use them for God, and seventeen percent wanted to learn more about the Holy Spirit (Chart 5).

When asked their spiritual goals in this study, the majority of the participants, 50 percent, said they wanted to grow spiritually (Chart 6). Their primary goal for the church followed a similar pattern, in that 46 percent of the participants said they wanted their local church to grow spiritually and serve in the gifts (Chart 7). When asked if they had personal daily devotions with the Lord, the majority of the participants, 58 percent, responded that they do; while 21 percent responded that they do not; 17 percent had no response; and 4 percent responded they sometimes have personal daily devotions (Chart 8).

The Holy Spirit

The first course topic was, "Who is the Holy Spirit?" In this section, a series of questions were asked to measure the students' understanding of the ministry of the Holy Spirit in general, and the baptism in the Holy Spirit in particular.

The Holy Spirit was described as a part of the Trinity by 38 percent of the respondents; as a "feeling" by 29 percent; and 33 percent did not respond (Chart 9). When asked about the personhood of the Holy Spirit, 46 percent responded He is a person; 21 percent responded that the Holy Spirit is a thing; 21 percent had no response; 8 percent said they could not explain; and 4 percent said they were not sure (Chart 10). Respondents indicated an uncertainty about the ministry of the Holy Spirit. Although 25 percent of the students responded that His ministry is to testify about Jesus, to lead, to guide, to comfort, and to strengthen believers, 59 percent simply did not respond (Chart 11). When asked where the Holy Spirit is, 50 percent responded that He is within; 8 percent responded everywhere; a significant proportion of attendees, 42 percent, did not respond (Chart 12).

The respondents did not have a clear perception of the baptism in the Holy Spirit; however, 62 percent offered their own definitions which ranged from power, 21 percent; to doing God's will, 17 percent; to salvation, 12 percent; to joy, love, and calmness, 12 percent; and 38 percent did not respond (Chart 13). In response to the question, "Who can receive the baptism in the Holy Spirit?" 38 percent said believers in the Lord Jesus Christ; while 33 percent said everyone and 29 percent did not respond (Chart 14). In response to the question, "Is the baptism in the Holy Spirit received at salvation, or is it a separate experience," 37 percent responded that the baptism is received as a separate experience while 21 percent said the baptism was received at conversion. The majority, 42 percent, did not respond (Chart 15).

The data from the pre-test questionnaire proved my pre-supposition that many Christians are well versed in the doctrine of God the Father and God the Son, but they are not as knowledgeable of the doctrine of God the Holy Spirit, so the instructional material was modified to meet the needs of the students. Each student was given a course syllabus. Course topics included: "Who is the Holy Spirit?"; "The Personality of the Holy Spirit"; "The Old Testament and the New Testament Witness of the Holy Spirit"; "The Baptism in the Holy Spirit"; and "Spiritual Gifts." A glimpse of selected renewal movements in church history from the Protestant Reformation in the sixteenth century to the Pentecostal and Charismatic Movement in the twentieth century provided an historical context for seeking renewal in this present age (see chapter 4 – The Renewal of the Church)

Spiritual Gifts

The second course topic was the utilization of spiritual gifts. Spiritual gifts are fundamental for renewing, reviving, and restoring the people of God.

The purpose of the gifts is *"to prepare God's people for works of service, so that the body of Christ may be built up until we all reach unity in the faith and in the knowledge of the Son of God and become mature, attaining to the whole measure of the fullness of Christ"* (Eph. 4:12). Believers need to discover their spiritual gifts so that they will be equipped to do the work of ministry effectively through the power of the Holy Spirit. I asked the participants in the study to define spiritual gifts in order to measure their understanding of the gifts. Of the twenty-four responses, 25 percent answered that gifts are given by the Holy Spirit to build up the church; 9 percent responded they are gifts used to bless others; the other responses included ministries, 4 percent; natural abilities, 4 percent; defined by the apostles and died with them, 4 percent; and do not know four percent (Chart 16). They were asked to list their gifts. Several gifts were listed by 25 percent of the respondents, while 25 percent did not know their gifts. Again, the majority of the participants, 50 percent, did not respond (Chart 17). When asked if they are using their spiritual gifts, 25 percent responded no, while 17 percent responded yes; 17 percent responded sometimes, and 41 percent did not respond (Chart 18). Their responses proved the need to teach on this important work of the Holy Spirit.

The intellectual model used for this section of the course was <u>Your Spiritual Gifts Can Help Your Church Grow</u> by C. Peter Wagner. Wagner contends, "Ignorance of spiritual gifts may be the chief cause of retarded church growth. It may also be at the root of much discouragement, insecurity, frustration and guilt that plagues many Christians and curtails their effectiveness for God"(Wagner 24). Wagner argues, "No local congregation will be what it should be, what Jesus prayed that it would be, what the Holy Spirit gifted it and empowered it to be, until it understands spiritual gifts" (Ibid 30).

Again, we are reminded that we cannot select our spiritual gifts. God is the giver of spiritual gifts, and He decides which gifts will be given to every regenerated Christian (Rom. 12:6; 1 Cor. 12:11; Eph. 4:11). The purpose of the gifts is to glorify God and to prepare God's people for service and witness for Christ (1 Pet. 4:11). The gifts are given to have a unifying effect upon the church (1 Cor. 12:12-13; Eph. 4:13), and they are given to enhance Christian maturity (Eph. 4:13). According to Tony Evans, "spiritual gifts are Holy Spirit empowered abilities given to the members of the body to facilitate the growth, edification and maturity of the church" (Evans 299).

The Greek word *pneumatikos* is translated as "spiritual." It always connotes the ideas of invisibility and power. It does not occur in the Septuagint or in the Gospels; it is in fact an after-Pentecost word (Vine 594). According to David Walker, "the word *pneumatick* employed in First Corinthians 12:1 is used to describe the gifts as 'things belonging to the Spirit' (Walker 2022). It is derived from *pneuma*, "spirit," which refers to the supernatural manifestations of the Holy Spirit. Lindsey Garmon contends,

The Greek word translated "gifts" is "charismata" (the singular is "charisma"). The root word is "charis" which means, "grace." Therefore, spiritual gifts are grace gifts or grace endowments that Christians receive from God in the form of abilities through which God desires to channel His energy and power as a means of strengthening the body and bringing glory to His name! (Garmon 7)

There are three key lists of spiritual gifts in the New Testament (Rom. 12:6-8; Eph. 4:11; and 1 Cor. 12:4-11). Each person of the Godhead participated in giving the gifts.

Spiritual Gifts		
MOTIVATIONAL (Rom. 12:3-8)	**MANIFESTATION (I Cor. 12:7-10,28)**	**MINISTRY (Eph. 4:11)**
Perceiver	Wisdom	Apostles
Server	Knowledge	Prophets
Teacher	Supernatural Faith	Evangelists
Exhorter	Healing	Pastors
Giver	Miracles	Teachers
Administrator	Prophecy	
Compassion	Discernment of Spirits	
	TONGUES	
	INTERPRETATION OF TONGUES	

- The gifts given by God the Father are for basic life purpose and motivation. They are perceiver, server, teacher, exhorter, giver, administrator, and compassion (Rom. 12:6-8; 1 Pet. 4:11).
- The gifts given by God the Son are ministry gifts, or "office gifts," given to facilitate and equip the Body of Christ. Many refer to these gifts as the five-fold ministry. They are apostles, prophets, evangelists, pastors and teachers (Eph. 4:7-16).
- The gifts given by God the Holy Spirit are manifestation gifts. They are word of wisdom, word of knowledge, faith, gifts of healings, workings of miracles, prophecy, discerning of spirits, different kinds of tongues, and interpretation of tongues (1 Cor. 12:4-11). This list is not meant to be exhaustive. In fact, Wagner lists 27 gifts in his book. He included celibacy, voluntary poverty, martyrdom, intercession, and deliverance (1 Cor. 7:13-14; Eph. 3, 1 Pet. 4). Wagner affirms that God is the giver of spiritual gifts.

The teaching on spiritual gifts comes directly from the Word of God. This gives us the assurance we need so we can say with confidence that it is truly God's way for his people to operate with one another. It is the way to do God's work, whether caring for each other, or learning more about the faith, or celebrating the resurrection of Jesus Christ, or reaching out to the lost with the message of God's love. It is the way to bring about the kind of church growth that builds the whole person and the whole body of Christ (Wagner 226).

Wagner's book provides an overview of the rediscovery of spiritual gifts in modern times, and a thorough presentation of the definition, purpose and use of the gifts. The participants were assigned chapters of his book to read for homework and were expected to come to class prepared to discuss the material and to ask questions.

To facilitate the participants' understanding of the role of the gifts in serving the church, I administered two spiritual gifts inventories. The first inventory based on the book, <u>How to Find Meaning and Fulfillment Through Understanding the Spiritual Gift Within You</u> by Larry Gilbert, was given the first week to help familiarize participants with a spiritual gifts inventory and to help them relax while building momentum for the course. I informed them that they would take another spiritual gifts inventory near the end of the course, and they could compare the two for similarities and differences in their responses as they gained more knowledge through the readings and lectures. Some of the participants were reluctant to answer the questions, so I explained, "There are no right or wrong answers. You should answer based on what you feel inside and not based on another person's expectation of you. Take your time, reflect, and be honest with yourself so that you experience the joy of discovering your gifts." Once they conquered the fear of answering incorrectly, they became excited as they worked through the inventory.

There was great interest in the subject matter.

Each week the participants listened attentively to the lectures as we studied the gifts. They were particularly interested in learning about the manifestation gifts in First Corinthians 12:4-11 so those gifts became the focus of the spiritual gifts section of the course. The nine manifestation gifts were studied by placing them in three categories as suggested by Dennis and Rita Bennett (Bennett 86):

- The Revelation Gifts (the power to know): Word of Knowledge, Word of Wisdom, and Discernment of Spirits.
- The Power Gifts (the power to do): Supernatural Faith, Healing, and Miracles.
- The Inspirational Gifts (the power to say): Tongues, Interpretation of Tongues, and Prophecy.

Since this was a new area of study for some of the participants, I wrote a brief definition for most of the gifts and cited biblical examples of each gift.

THE NINE MANIFESTATION GIFTS OF THE HOLY SPIRIT

To one there is given through the Spirit the message of wisdom, to another the message of knowledge by means of the same Spirit, to another faith by the same Spirit, to another gifts of healing by that one Spirit, to another miraculous powers, to another prophecy, to another distinguishing between spirits, to another speaking in different kinds of tongues, and still another the interpretation of tongues. All these are the work of one and the same Spirit, and he gives them to each one, just as he determines (I Cor. 12:8-11).

Scriptural References for
The First Category of the Manifestation Gifts
<u>*Revelation Gifts*</u>
(1 Cor. 12:8-10b)

Word of Knowledge
- *Acts 5:1-10*
- *Acts 9:10-12, 17*
- *Acts 10:17-23*

Word of Wisdom
- *Matt. 22:15-22*
- *Luke21:12-15*
- *Acts 6:8-10*

Discernment of Spirits
- *1 Kings 22:17; 19:23*
- *Matt. 16:16, 17*
- *Acts 16:16-18*

Word of Knowledge

God supernaturally reveals information about a person or circumstance of the past, present or future. These facts are not learned through research or study; rather, the Holy Spirit quickens the spirit of the person with the knowledge to speak His Word.

Biblical Examples of a Word of Knowledge

- The King of Assyria's defeat was foretold (Isa. 37:6-7).

- Ananias and Sapphira's lie to the Holy Spirit was uncovered (Acts 5:1-10).

- Peter was instructed by the Holy Spirit to go with the men sent by Cornelius (Acts 10:17-22).

Word of Wisdom

The person with this gift is given the answer to a problem or concern, but it does not come from natural intelligence or academic training. God, the Holy Spirit, supernaturally reveals the information. It is "knowing" in your spirit that God has supernaturally given to you the answer that is needed. A Word of Wisdom tells the person how to use the Word of Knowledge in a given situation, to bring praise and glory to God, and to edify the persons.

Biblical Examples of Word of Wisdom

- Jesus responded to the Pharisees when questioned about paying taxes to Caesar (Matt. 22:17).

- Jesus promised to give wisdom to those who are persecuted for righteousness (Luke 21:12-15).
- Stephen was given the gift of wisdom (Acts 6:8-10).

Discernment of Spirits

God, the Holy Spirit supernaturally reveals the presence of good or demonic spirits. This revelation looks beyond one's physical appearance and speech to discern the spirit that is in charge. Discernment of Spirits is crucial in purifying the church, in spiritual warfare and deliverance ministry. It is the "watchful eye" of the Body of Christ.

Biblical Examples of Discernment of Spirits

- Peter's confession of Christ (Matt. 16: 16,17).

- Paul confronted the evil spirit in Elymas (Acts 13:8-11).

- Paul called out the evil spirit in a slave girl (Acts 16:16-18).

Scriptural References for

The Second Category of the Manifestation Gifts

Power Gifts
1 Cor. 12:9-10a

Supernatural Faith

- Joshua 14:10-15

- John 20:10-15

- Matt. 15:21-28

Healing

- Acts 9:32-35

- Acts 14:8-10

- Acts 28:8, 9

Miracles

- Joshua 10:12-14

- 1 Kings 17:17-24

- Acts 9:36-42

Supernatural Faith

Supernatural faith is the unwavering belief that God will do what He said in His Word. This faith cannot be shaken by trouble, hardship, sickness or unemployment. It conquers all negative thoughts such as quit, can't, impossible, failure, scared, etc. Every time the enemy tells you what you can't do and what you can't have, supernatural faith rises up on the inside and tells you what you can do and what you can have by the power of the Holy Spirit. You will have Holy Ghost boldness to tell people, "I am not worried; I BELIEVE GOD!"

Biblical Examples of Supernatural Faith

- Caleb waited 45 years for God to fulfill His promise (Josh. 14:10-15).

- Mary Magdalene's devotion to Jesus overshadowed her human limitations (John 20:10-15).

- The Canaanite mother knew that Jesus was the only person who could help her daughter (Matt. 15:21-28).

Healing

God supernaturally heals the physical and emotional ailments of His people without medication. God is not against medication. He chooses whether the healing will take place supernaturally (a gift of healing) or through medication, surgery or other forms of medical treatment. Much prayer, faith, and belief in the Word of God must accompany this gift.

Biblical Examples of Healing

- Aeneas, a paralytic for eight years, walked (Acts 9:32-35).

- A crippled man jumped up and walked (Acts 14:8-10).

- The father of the chief official and others were healed (Acts 28:8-9.

Miracles

God supernaturally intervenes in the life of His people by performing acts of miracles that defy human reasoning and bring glory to His name. It pleases God to do the "impossible" for His people while destroying the works of Satan.

Biblical Examples of Miracles

- The sun and moon obeyed (Josh. 10:12-14).

- A son was returned to his mother alive (I Kings 17: 17-24).

- A woman was released from death (Acts 9:36-42).

Scriptural References for the

third Category of the Manifestation Gifts

<u>Inspirational Gifts</u>
(1 Cor. 12:10)

Tongues

- Acts 2:1-12
- Acts 10:44-46
- Acts 19:1-6

INTERPRETATION OF TONGUES

- Rom. 8:26-27
- 1 Cor. 14:26-28
- 1 Cor. 14:5

PROPHECY

- luke 2:36-38
- Acts 21:8-9
- 1 Cor. 14:1-4

Tongues (glossalalia)

Tongues are the supernatural gift of the Holy Spirit that empowers believers to speak to God in another language that they have not studied or learned. This language may be a known language (Acts 2:7-12) or the language of angels (I Cor. 13:1). Tongues bypass the thoughts and vocabulary of the natural mind to speak directly to God in the spirit .

Biblical Examples of Speaking in Tongues

- Believers were baptized in the Holy Spirit (Acts 2:1-12).

- Gentiles were baptized in the Holy Spirit (Acts 10:44-46).

- Twelve disciples received the gift of tongues (Acts19:1-6).)

Interpretation of Tongues

Interpretation of tongues is the supernatural ability to translate the tongues that have been spoken by no more than three persons. This knowledge is not learned from anyone. It is a quickening in your spirit that overflows in your speaking, sometimes without realizing what you are saying, to interpret the message so that God will be praised, and the Body of Christ will be edified.

Biblical Examples of Interpretation of Tongues

- The Holy Spirit interprets believer's prayer language (Rom. 8:26-27).

- The importance of interpretation of tongues in the corporate worship experience (I Cor.14:5).

- The proper use of this gift in corporate worship is explained (I Cor. 14: 26-28).

Prophecy

"Prophecy is a special gift that enables a believer to bring a word or revelation directly from God under the impulse of the Holy Spirit (I Cor. 14:24-25,29-31). It is not the delivery of a previously prepared sermon. In both the Old Testament and the New Testament, prophecy is not primarily foretelling the future but proclaiming God's will and exhorting and encouraging God's people to righteousness, faithfulness and endurance….all prophecy must be tested for the genuineness and truth (I Cor. 14:29,32; I Thess. 5:20-21) by asking whether it conforms to God's Word (John 4:1), whether it promotes godly living (I Tim. 6:3), and whether it is uttered by one who is sincerely living under Christ's Lordship (I Cor. 12:3)" (Full Life Study Bible).

Biblical Examples of Prophecy

- Deborah, a prophetess led Israel (Judg. 4:4).

- Anna prophesied over the baby Jesus (Luke 2:36-38).

- Philip's daughters prophesied (Acts 21:8-9).

Remember, we cannot choose our gifts. The gifts are divinely given by the Holy Spirit for the good of the Body of Christ. Therefore, there should never be any jealousy, envy, boasting or competing for "certain" gifts. The Corinthians were guilty of these charges. It is not coincidental that right in the middle of First Corinthians 12 and 14, which speak of spiritual gifts, the Holy Spirit wrote the great love chapter of the Bible, First Corinthians 13. He did so to reveal to believers that love is the greatest gift of all. If we allow Satan to cause us to become puffed up, prideful, arrogant or to think more highly of ourselves than we ought because of our spiritual gifts, then we are no longer acting in love; consequently, we are not edifying the Body of Christ. The gifts are meant to unite the Body of Christ in love and lead us to spiritual maturity. We should never be divided based on the gift of tongues or any of the other gifts. If a congregation is blessed to have all of the gifts in use in their local church and they do not love one another, the gifts are not profitable. Christians should be content with the gift(s) God has given us, and use them to renew the church. David Cho struggled with wanting "certain" gifts but came to the conclusion that he must use the gifts God has given him:

> When I first received the Holy Spirit, I prayed blindly for more of the gifts that were most popular, the gift of healing, for the gift of the word of wisdom and for the gift of the word of knowledge. Though I prayed at length with many tears, the anticipated gifts were not forthcoming.

Though it seemed that those gifts appeared for a while, I did not have an outstanding flow of those gifts of the Spirit continually. Instead, gifts I did not ask for or pay much attention to began to appear in my personal life and ministry like new shoots of grass sprouting on the earth (Cho 143-144).

God wants us to trust Him to give us the gifts He determines. Then once we receive the gifts, we must have the faith to use them to serve the Body of Christ. Dennis and Rita Bennett recalled an example of how God used a stranger who was praying in tongues to witness to an unbeliever. A young man attended a Full Gospel church in Oregon. He was a Christian, but his new bride from Japan practiced Buddhism. One evening they were praying together at the altar at the end of a church service. He prayed to God, and she prayed to the idol god, Buddha. Little did she know that the true and living God would use this moment to transform her life:

> Next to them was kneeling a middle-aged woman, a housewife from the community. As this woman began to pray out loud in tongues, suddenly the Japanese bride seized her husband's arm.

> "Listen!" She whispered in excitement. "This woman speaks to me in Japanese! She says to me, 'You have tried Buddha, and he does you no good. Why don't you try Jesus Christ?' She

does not speak to me in ordinary Japanese language; she speaks temple Japanese and uses my whole Japanese name, which no one in this country knows!" It is not surprising that the young lady became a Christian (Bennett 86).

What a wonderful testimony to the power of the Lord Jesus Christ to save those who are lost! God spoke through an ordinary woman who spoke in tongues to transform the life of this young Japanese woman. Hallelujah!

As the series progressed, some participants shared testimonies of their experiences in receiving the baptism in the Holy Spirit; others stated they had attended revivals in which the evangelist flowed in the gift of prophecy, word of wisdom and word of knowledge. One lady shared her experience of being supernaturally healed of cancer, another lady said her vocal cords were healed, and she was able to sing again. After hearing the testimonies, the students wanted to learn more about the gifts. The personal testimonies generated an excitement and enthusiasm unmatched by scholarly research, which is consistent with the Word of God, *"They overcame by the blood of the Lamb and by the word of their testimony"* (Rev. 12:11).

At this point in the course, the participants took the second spiritual gifts inventory, the Wagner-Modified Houts Questionnaire. Having taken another spiritual gifts inventory earlier in the course, the participants were much more comfortable and confident in answering and scoring this inventory.

For some, the questionnaire confirmed known gifts. However, many of them discovered their gifts for the first time.

Based on their newly discovered gifts, I challenged the participants to come out of their comfort zone and serve in ministries that matched their spiritual gifts. The pastor of the site church indicated he would use this information as a tool to match people with their spiritual gifts. He said that he had already asked some people to serve in a particular area of ministry, and the results of their spiritual gifts test confirmed he was on target. One of the ladies said, "Pastor asked me to serve as an officer of the church, but I did not want to do it. Now I see, based on my gifts, that is where I should serve. I guess I'll stop resisting and accept the position." It is a joy to know that the utilization of spiritual gifts is a key component to church renewal.

Spiritual renewal will take place in churches that are stagnant and in decline if they are open to receive the baptism in the Holy Spirit and use their spiritual gifts. The people must hunger and thirst for righteousness and pray fervently. The church can learn from renewal movements of the past, how the Holy Spirit breathes new life into the church when the people are committed to live holy before God.

When the first century believers were baptized in the Holy Spirit, they changed the course of history, and today over two thousand years later, their story is still being told. God placed their story in His Word as a testimony of His power and a reminder that the same blessing is available to every regenerated

Christian today.

Baptism in the Holy Spirit is the first essential ingredient for renewal of the church, and spiritual gifts are the second essential ingredient for renewal. According to Leith Anderson, "Spiritual gifts have been both a cause and an effect of spiritual renewal as ministry has been liberated from the clergy and increasingly become the privilege and responsibility of the laity" (Anderson 129). All believers are ministers of the Gospel of Jesus Christ. Whether we serve in the ordained ministry or the lay ministry, we have a ministry to fulfill as we make disciples for Jesus Christ and teach them to use their gifts in the local church to glorify God.

Summary

Once the class discovered their spiritual gifts, they were encouraged to seek new opportunities for ministry within the local church and to begin an evangelism program. The discovery of spiritual gifts created a new vitality in the group. The course:

- Restored their hope.
- Generated a greater desire to practice the spiritual discipline of prayer, Bible study and Scripture reading.
- Provided an opportunity for believers to learn and grow together.
- Opened new avenues for ministry in the local churches that were represented in the group.

Their enthusiasm will become contagious as Christians work in the area of ministry for which the Holy Spirited has gifted us.

Most of the participants moved to a new level of spiritual maturity and were able to identify what they had previously labeled "a feeling within" motivated them to attend this study. Namely, they wanted to experience personal and corporate renewal. When asked whether Christians need to be renewed in the Holy Spirit, 71 percent responded yes; while four percent responded they did not know; and 25 percent did not respond (Chart 19). In response to the question, "How will renewal help them personally and the church corporately?", 50 percent responded renewal will bring unity, new life and growth; eight percent did not know and 42 percent did not respond (Chart 20). When asked, "What steps can be taken to bring renewal?", 25 percent responded prayer, Bible study, reading the Word, fasting, revival and commitment; while 75 percent did not respond (Chart 21). The participants were asked to list other thoughts or comments they wanted to share concerning the course. The majority, 88 percent, had no response; while eight percent said they wanted to know their gifts; and four percent said they had no response "at this time"

Renewal will come by prayer, holy living and following the biblical principles of receiving the baptism in the Holy Spirit and using spiritual gifts to glorify God and build up the church. Personal renewal will lead the church to corporate renewal, which will be manifested in many ways:

- A greater love for God
- Agape love for one another
- Spiritual growth
- New converts
- New ministries
- Evangelism
- Social reform
- Numerical growth

PRAYER

(Supplication)

Dear God,

Thank You for the blessings of the baptism in the Holy Spirit and the gifts of the Holy Spirit. My supplication to You is that all born-again believers will receive these blessings and walk in the fullness of the power of the Holy Spirit. Holy God, please renew Your Church in our day. I pray in Jesus' name. Amen. (Phil. 4:6).

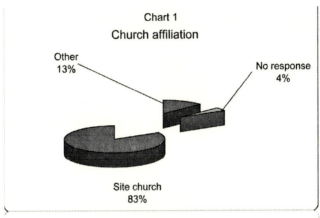

Chart 1
Church affiliation

Other
13%

No response
4%

Site church
83%

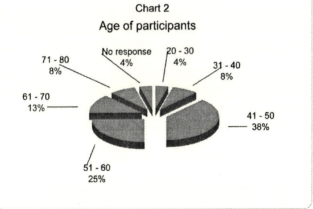

Chart 2
Age of participants

71 - 80
8%

No response
4%

20 - 30
4%

31 - 40
8%

61 - 70
13%

41 - 50
38%

51 - 60
25%

Note: Data is from Pre-Test Questionnaire.
N = 24

151

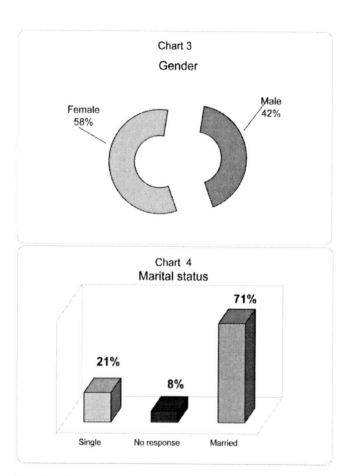

Chart 3
Gender

Female 58%
Male 42%

Chart 4
Marital status

71%

21%

8%

Single   No response   Married

Note: Data is from Pre-Test Questionnaire.
N = 24

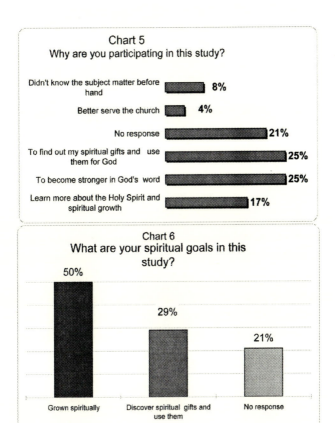

Chart 5
Why are you participating in this study?

Didn't know the subject matter before hand	8%
Better serve the church	4%
No response	21%
To find out my spiritual gifts and use them for God	25%
To become stronger in God's word	25%
Learn more about the Holy Spirit and spiritual growth	17%

Chart 6
What are your spiritual goals in this study?

Grown spiritually	Discover spiritual gifts and use them	No response
50%	29%	21%

Note: Data is from Pre-Test Questionnaire.
N = 24

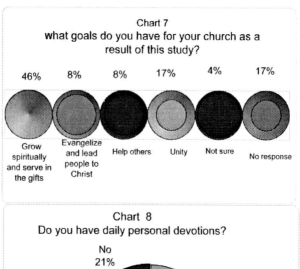

Chart 7
what goals do you have for your church as a result of this study?

46%	8%	8%	17%	4%	17%
Grow spiritually and serve in the gifts	Evangelize and lead people to Christ	Help others	Unity	Not sure	No response

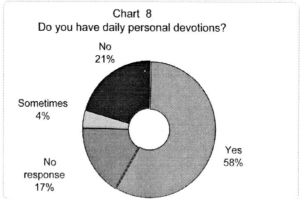

Chart 8
Do you have daily personal devotions?

No 21%

Sometimes 4%

No response 17%

Yes 58%

Note: Data is from Pre-Test Questionnaire.
N = 24

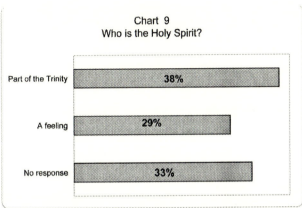

Chart 9
Who is the Holy Spirit?

Part of the Trinity	38%
A feeling	29%
No response	33%

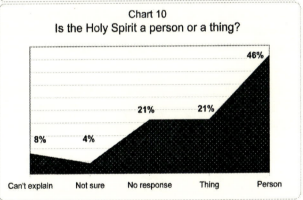

Chart 10
Is the Holy Spirit a person or a thing?

Can't explain	Not sure	No response	Thing	Person
8%	4%	21%	21%	46%

Note: Data is from Pre-Test Questionnaire.
N = 24

Chart 11
What is the ministry of the Holy Spirit?

Convict and deliver 4%
Praise God 4%
Not sure 8%
Testify about Jesus, lead, guide, comfort 25%
No response 59%

Chart 12

Where is the Holy Spirit?

50%
8%
42%

Within me
Everywhere
No response

Note: Data is from Pre-Test Questionnaire.
N = 24

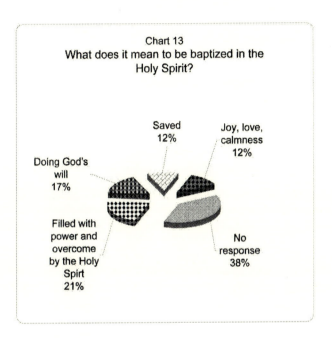

Chart 13
What does it mean to be baptized in the
Holy Spirit?

Saved
12%

Joy, love,
calmness
12%

Doing God's
will
17%

Filled with
power and
overcome
by the Holy
Spirt
21%

No
response
38%

Note: Data is from Pre-Test Questionnaire.
N = 24

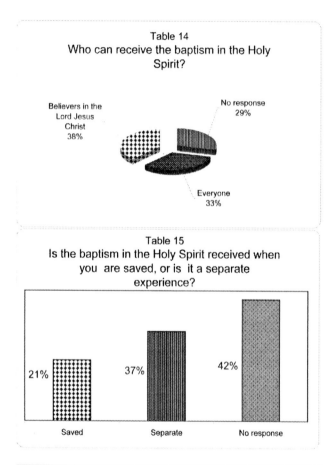

Table 14
Who can receive the baptism in the Holy Spirit?

Believers in the Lord Jesus Christ 38%

No response 29%

Everyone 33%

Table 15
Is the baptism in the Holy Spirit received when you are saved, or is it a separate experience?

21% Saved

37% Separate

42% No response

Note: Data is from Pre-Test Questionnaire.
N = 24

Chart 16
Define the gifts of the Holy Spirit

- Natural abilities — 4%
- Gifts used to bless other — 9%
- Gifts given by the Holy Spirit to build up the church — 25%
- No response — 50%
- Ministries — 4%
- Defined by the Apostle and died with them — 4%
- Don't know — 4%

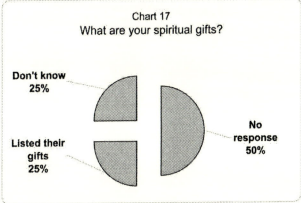

Chart 17
What are your spiritual gifts?

- Don't know 25%
- Listed their gifts 25%
- No response 50%

Note: Data is from Pre-Test Questionnaire.
N = 24

Table 18
Are you using your spiritual gifts

Note: Data is from Pre-Test Questionnaire.
N = 24

Chart 19
Do Christians Need to be Renewed in the Holy Spirit?

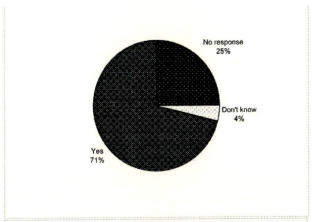

Chart 20
How will renewal help you personally and the church corporately?

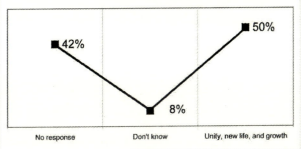

Note: Data is from Pre-Test Questionnaire.
N = 24

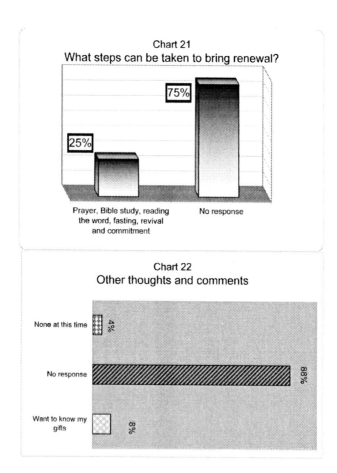

Chart 21
What steps can be taken to bring renewal?

75%

25%

Prayer, Bible study, reading the word, fasting, revival and commitment

No response

Chart 22
Other thoughts and comments

None at this time — 4%

No response — 88%

Want to know my gifts — 8%

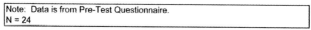

Note: Data is from Pre-Test Questionnaire.
N = 24

CHAPTER 6

<u>THE ANALYSIS</u>

"Do not conform any longer to the pattern of this world, but be transformed by the renewing of your mind. Then you will be able to test and approve what God's will is – his good, pleasing and perfect will" (Rom. 12:2).

My thesis for this project was that renewal of the church would come through the baptism in the Holy Spirit and the utilization of spiritual gifts. I designed an instructional program to test the validity of this theological and theoretical supposition. Through the use of a pre-test, post-test, and course evaluation, I was able to measure the participants' understanding of the subject matter, ascertain their goals for the study, and evaluate the effectiveness of the study.

The pre-test instrument revealed that many of the participants were not well versed in the ministry of the Holy Spirit in general, and in the baptism in the Holy Spirit and spiritual gifts in particular. The students participated in the study because they desired renewal within their personal life and in the life of the church, and they wanted to learn more about the subject matter.

I administered a post-test and a course evaluation form the last night of class to measure the effectiveness of the study and to measure spiritual growth that took place as a result of the course experience. I did not seek to measure whether the participants received the baptism in the Holy Spirit because the goal was to provide an historical teaching on the baptism in the Holy Spirit, and to teach the participants how to trust God to empower His people. I did, however, use the post-test instrument and course evaluation form to measure the participants' understanding of spiritual gifts.

The number of participants who completed the post-test was significantly lower than the 24 participants who completed the pre-test that was administered at the beginning of the course. The low response, in all probability, was due to the tremendous amount of enthusiasm and interaction among the participants on the last night of class. The celebratory atmosphere did not lend itself to completion of forms. However, thirteen persons did respond to the post-test, and twelve persons completed the course evaluation form.

The analysis of the pre-test and post-test instruments proved the participants experienced spiritual growth by the end of the course. From the responses, the participants felt they had met their learning goals and gained a wealth of information on the ministry of the Holy Spirit. The responses and the course evaluations proved that the lectures, teaching style, and course materials enhanced the effectiveness of the course.

Persons who participated in this study were looking for ways to become more involved in their church. They did not confine their Christianity to the Sunday morning worship experience. Rather, they followed the pattern of persons who serve in successful churches. George Barna observed,

> Individuals who became regulars at successful churches understood that real Christianity is not a spectator sport. It is a participatory, hands-on way of life. They were compelled by calling and desire, rather than ritualistic obligation, to play a role in the work of the church. They recognized that just being in the right place at the appointed time was an empty demonstration of obedience that lacked meaning. Their goal was to be Christian by living in accordance with the principles Christ taught. They strove to be the church, at all times, in all places (Barna 69-70).

At the end of the course, some of the participants agreed to continue meeting together in a small group setting and to hold one another accountable for using their gifts to edify the Body of Christ. They felt they had been renewed and had an eagerness to study God's Word, to witness to others and to live out the faith in holiness.

I have been blessed immensely by having the opportunity to share God's Word with these wonderful saints. The work was rewarding and challenging. It was rewarding in that I was continually filled with the Holy Spirit as I taught the Word of God, shared personal testimonies, listened to others, and interacted with the group. It was challenging in that I wanted to give my best to the Lord and to the participants each week. My resolve was to trust the Holy Spirit to teach through me, so that all of the people would be blessed.

RECOMMENDATIONS FOR FUTURE INSTRUCTIONS ON THIS SUBJECT

- Spiritual preparation for instructor:

(A) Pray for the baptism in the Holy Spirit. If you have already been baptized in the Spirit, pray for the filling of the Holy Spirit daily.

(B) Pray for God's divine direction in preparing to minister to His people.

(C) Always be prepared, but allow the Holy Spirit to lead you as you teach. Adapt to His leading.

(D) Be open with the group. Let them know you are a real person. You do not have all of the answers, but you are in touch with the One who does.

(E) Let your belief in the course content be evident as you teach and talk with them weekly.

(F) Encourage the participants to use their spiritual gifts in ministries in which the Holy Spirit has equipped them to serve.

(G) Pray for them daily by name, and always be available after class for prayer and conversation.

(H) Learn and grow with them.

- <u>Devote more time to teaching on the baptism in the Holy Spirit</u>. Although this topic was discussed in detail, it is my opinion that more time should have been devoted to impress upon the believers the need to pray for, yearn for, and expect Jesus to baptize them in His Spirit. I would reemphasize that those who have been baptized in the Holy Spirit need to pray for the filling of the Holy Spirit daily, to be empowered to live for Jesus.

- <u>Stress the use of spiritual gifts</u>. The participants should be strongly encouraged to move from their comfort zone of service in the church and serve in areas of ministry for which the Holy Spirit has gifted them. Accountability to God, to self, the pastor, and other saints is highly recommended.

- <u>Change the required text</u>. The required text, <u>Your Spiritual Gifts Can Help Your Church</u>

Grow by C. Peter Wagner, was useful. Although he identified four kinds of church growth; his emphasis was primarily on numerical church growth. I do not want to undermine the importance of church growth, however, I think we need to focus on both spiritual growth and numerical growth. Once the people grow spiritually and fulfill the Great Commission (Matt. 28:18-20), numerical growth will follow. I would recommend that the instructor take advantage of the latest scholarship in the area and include two books that have been in print for sometime, The Holy Spirit and You by Dennis and Rita Bennett and The Holy Spirit, My Senior Partner by David Yonggi Cho. Both of these books provide a thorough overview of the ministry of the Holy Spirit, including the baptism in the Holy Spirit and the use of spiritual gifts. In addition, in the study of motivational gifts, I would recommend Discover Your God-Given Gifts by Don and Katie Fortune, which focuses on the gifts in Romans 12. This book would give the participants great insight into their own personality and how to interact with others based on their motivational gifts.

- Administer one spiritual gifts inventory. I administered two inventories within a six-week period. The purpose was for the students to use these two tools for comparative analysis. They were to compare the responses of the first inventory, which was taken at the beginning of the course, with their responses to the second inventory at the end of the course, to measure whether they consistently identified the same gifts or if they had discovered additional gifts as a result of the study. This goal was not fully met. Perhaps a better method would have been to administer one inventory and recommend that participants re-take the same inventory at the end of the course and again in six months.

- <u>Limit the class size and keep a prayer journal</u>. In order to facilitate greater interaction between the instructor and the students, the class size should be limited to ten persons. Participants should keep a prayer journal during the course and continue journaling for six months after the course to measure their spiritual growth. At the end of the six months, they would re-take the same spiritual gifts inventory as recommended above.

- <u>Record each class</u>. Audio and videotapes should be made of each class. Many of the participants asked for tapes to use in their quiet time and to share with others. The tapes would also serve as a tool for course evaluation.

Summary

An analysis of the case study revealed that Christians want to learn and grow spiritually. As more courses are offered on the ministry of the Holy Spirit, I believe we will see a resurgence of church renewal. We need to pray intentionally that God will empower us to keep our spiritual fervor, to resist sin, and to live holy so that our Christian witness will impact the world in which we live.

PRAYER

(Sustains)

> Everlasting Father,
>
> My prayer is that You will come quickly and renew Your Church. I shall pray continually and hold fast my profession of faith without wavering, because I know that You are faithful. Your Word sustains me, and I wait patiently for the manifestation of a renewed, holy Church that will not compromise Your Word. In Jesus' name I pray. Amen. (Heb. 10:23, 35-36).

The final chapter of this book will focus on the authority of prayer in the personal lives of Christians and in the life of the church universal.

CHAPTER 7

THE POWER OF PRAYER

"Be joyful always, pray continually."
(1 Thess. 5:16,17)

The world is looking at the church to see if it will provide the leadership that is so desperately needed. The church must stand for righteousness and refuse to compromise the Gospel of Jesus Christ (Rom. 1:16). If the church is going to reverse the downward spiral of societal decline, it must be rooted and grounded in the Word of God and lead the world to Jesus Christ. Jesus left a legacy of honorable leadership for the church to follow. David McKenna offers an excellent analysis of Jesus Christ's leadership. "By experiencing the Incarnation for ourselves, we learn that Christian leaders are different in 'being' as well as 'doing.' Our Incarnational 'being' is to embody the Spirit of Christ; our Incarnational 'doing' is to empower His people" (McKenna 16). As the Body of Christ seeks to follow Jesus' honorable model for leadership, they must be committed to prayer, be baptized in the Holy Spirit, and use spiritual gifts. Jesus was committed to a life of prayer. Intimacy with the Father was more important to Jesus than anything else. He came to do the Father's will, and the only way to know the Father's will was to seek Him in prayer.

The Prayer Life of Jesus

Jesus loved to pray. He left the disciples early in the morning before sunrise and went to a solitary placed to pray (Mark 1:35). In the evening, after ministering to the masses, He often sent the disciples away, and He withdrew to a quiet place to commune with the Father (Mark 6:46-47). He sought out seasons of refreshing through solitary communions with the Father (Luke 5:15-16); and He often prayed all night (Luke 6:12). Jesus always prayed before performing miracles and ministering to the people (Mark 6:41; John 11:41-42). In the Sermon on the Mount, He taught the disciples and the multitudes how to pray (Matt. 6:5-13; 7:7-8; Luke 11:1-4). On the night of His betrayal, Jesus prayed the high priestly prayer, which included believers not yet born (John 17:1-26). In the Garden of Gethsemane, He surrendered His will to the Father through prayer (Luke 22:41-42). Jesus even interceded for His persecutors when hanging on the cross and asked the Father to forgive them (Luke 23:34). From Jesus' incarnation to His crucifixion, Jesus placed a high priority on prayer, and He did not allow anything or anyone to interfere with His quality time with the Father.

After Jesus' ascension, the disciples and the believers followed His model of praying continually. God heard their prayers and on the day of Pentecost sent the Holy Spirit to baptize them and empower them for ministry (Acts 2:1-13). Some time later, Peter and John were arrested for preaching in the name of Jesus. Upon their release, they went to the believers and shared their experience. In a spirit of unity, the believers prayed unto God for boldness to proclaim the Gospel message and perform miracles in the name of Jesus. *"After they prayed, the place where they were meeting was shaken. And they were all filled with the Holy Spirit and spoke the word of God boldly"* (Acts 4:31).

Prayer is one of the most important privileges of the Christian life. It is as essential to the Christian life as breathing is to the natural life. Through prayer, we are strengthened to live victoriously. Prayer opens the door and takes us from the outer courts into the personal, private chamber where the Most High dwells. When we enter the secret place of the Most High, we experience the beauty of the holiness of God. David said, *"One thing I ask of the Lord, this is what I seek: that I may dwell in the house of the Lord all the days of my life, to gaze upon the beauty of the Lord and to seek Him in His temple"* (Ps. 27:4). David simply wanted to be in the presence of the Lord and bask in the joy of being in the secret place of the Most High. It is there that heaven and earth bow and submit to His will. It is there, in the secret place, where God shelters us from the storms and builds a haven of rest for us in the midst of chaos.

In the Old Testament, the Hebrew verb for prayer is *palal*. It means "to pray, to intervene." This word occurs 84 times in the Old Testament. It expresses the idea of "interceding for, praying in behalf of" (Nu. 21:7). This verb emphasizes that prayer is basically communication, which always has to be two-way in order to be real (Vine 185).

In the New Testament, the Greek verb for prayer is *proseuchomai*. It means "to pray" and is always used in reference to prayer to God. It is the most frequently used word in this respect, especially in the synoptic gospels (Matthew, Mark, Luke) and Acts (once in Rom. 8:26; Eph. 6:18; Phil. 1:9; 1 Tim. 2:8; Heb. 13:18; Jude v. 20) (Ibid480).

In the Old Testament and the New Testament we see that effective prayer requires discipline. Through prayer, God offers divine direction, forgiveness, love, wisdom, encouragement, peace, and a wealth of blessings in the way that is needed most by those who are praying. Prayer then becomes the springboard for experiencing the abundant life and effectiveness in ministry.

In 1986 I attended a weekly Bible study at a small church in Cambridge, Massachusetts. (This church was not my home church). The pastor was a spirit-filled man of God who had a passion for prayer. God gave him a vision that the church was to host a revival and invite a well-known pastor from Washington, D.C. to minister. In the natural, it was not financially feasible for this little church to act on the vision, but the pastor moved in the supernatural realm and believed that it was time for the church to believe God for what seemed to be impossible. He called together a core group of people to pray for the revival. (Most of the core group was made up of persons from other local churches). The pastor said that the success of Billy Graham's ministry was due in large part to the power of prayer. In that, before Graham went into a city to preach, he sent a team ahead of him to pray and fast and to prepare the atmosphere for the receptivity of the preaching of God's holy Word. The pastor asked the core group to fast and pray at designated times in the home, to come together for corporate prayer several nights a week leading up to the revival, and to continue to pray during the revival. We prayed for the evangelist, salvation for the unsaved, reconciliation for the backsliders, good attendance each night, and for the resources to meet the financial needs of the revival.

I was so excited! I had just begun my seminary studies, and I felt privileged to be a part of pulling down the strongholds of Satan and believing God for the miraculous. The ten-member core group faithfully adhered to the covenant of prayer we had established. The evangelist agreed to come, and by the time the revival started, we knew the power of the Holy Spirit was present. Every night, the church was filled to capacity. People stood for hours in worship and to hear the Word of God. God answered all of our prayers. Souls were saved; backsliders returned to the Lord; many rededicated their lives to the Lord; relationships were restored; and yes, all of the financial obligations were met. Praise the Lord! Is there anything too difficult for God? No, not if we pray, seek His face, believe and stand on His Word.

I believe the success of this revival moved the congregation of that little Baptist church to a new level of faith. Many years later, the pastor is still a visionary. He was successful in bringing an international evangelist to the church for two consecutive years. The financial expense was great, but God's grace is sufficient. People gathered from all over the greater Boston metroplex and beyond to attend those meetings. Leadership that is devoted to pray and follow the will of God will always hear from God and triumph over adversity. Charles Stanley affirms, "Every time we pray to God, seeking His will, there are two things He wants to show us. He wants to show us Himself (Phil. 3:7-8) and He wants to show us what He is able to do (John 15:16). Is there anything greater than seeking God and knowing His power?" (Stanley 13).

It is essential that Christians cultivate an intimate relationship with God. Every Christian needs to have an unshakable faith in Jesus Christ and pray according to Jesus' directions to us in the Holy Bible. We live in the information age, where so many people are seeking god, but not the God of the Holy Bible. So much emphasis is placed on tolerance, ecumenical fellowship and participation in inter-faith organizations that it is easy to be deceived by false doctrine and praying to idol gods.

Joel S. Goldsmith was hailed as one of America's greatest Christian mystics, yet he argues that there are many ways to seek God:

> Every person who has known dissatisfaction, incompleteness, and frustration will some day learn that there is only one missing link in his entire chain of harmonious living. That is the practice of the presence of God—consciously, daily and hourly, abiding in some great spiritual truth of scripture, and it makes no difference which scripture: Christian, Hebrew, Hindu, Buddhist, Taoist, or Moslem. The word of God, given to man through inspired saints, sages, seers, or revelators – this is what we need, in any language, from any country, just as long as it is universal truth (Goldsmith 11).

How can a person be acclaimed a great Christian when he expounded false doctrine? The Word of God warned against such teaching (2 Tim. 4:3-4). Goldsmith's teaching in this area is diametrically opposed to the Word of God. Christians must remember that first, there is only one way to the Father and it is through Jesus Christ, the Son of God (John 14:6). Second, all prayer is to be directed to the Father in the name of Jesus Christ (John 16:23-24). And third, the Holy Spirit is the only author of Scripture. There is no substitute for Christian Scripture: *"Above all, you must understand that no prophecy of Scripture came about by the prophet's own interpretation. For prophecy never had its origin in the will of man, but men spoke from God as they were carried along by the Holy Spirit (2 Pet.*

1:20,21). It is imperative that Christians pray to the Father in the name of Jesus Christ.

The topic of church growth is discussed in most evangelical settings today. People are looking for new ways to grow their church, but they often overlook the foundation to church growth, which is prayer. The growth of the church in the twenty-first century will depend in large measure on the prayer life of Christian leaders and born-again believers. Andrew Evans, senior pastor of the Assembly of God church in Paradise, Adelaida, Australia, recounts how the Lord revealed this great truth in his life and ministry.

Evans served God as a missionary in Papua, New Guinea, for seven years before his denomination called him to pastor a local congregation of educated parishioners in Adelaida. He felt intimidated by the assignment but worked diligently on every sermon. At the end of the first year, to his dismay, the church attendance had decreased from 200 to 150 persons. His confidence was shattered, yet he looked for several ways to insure church growth. After reading a book entitled <u>How to have a Soul Winning Church</u>, in which the author's church grew from 17 to 2,000 through door knocking, Evans began a door-to-door campaign. They knocked on one thousand doors and witnessed to people, but not one of those persons came to church. He felt like a failure. Next, he decided to bring in a renowned minister with a healing ministry. The church expended a great deal of money on publicity, banners and other related expenses, but at the end of the meetings, only 23 persons made decisions for Christ, and none of them came forward. They simply filled out the registration card. Evans counted this as another failure. But he was not defeated. He thought that since he did not have the gift of evangelism, he would invite an evangelist to join the staff, and that person would be responsible for church growth. The evangelist he invited declined. Evans saw this as another failure. In fact, every idea failed, and attendance continued to decrease. One day one of the parishioners came to see Evans and confided that his wife was going to leave him. He asked the pastor, "What should I do?" At this point, Evans was broken and responded, "I don't know." Nevertheless, he told the man that they should fast and pray and meet in the church on Saturday for prayer. The man agreed. During the prayer meeting, God spoke to Evans and told him that he wanted them to meet every Saturday for fasting and prayer. Evans agreed, but he told God that he would have to tell the man himself. God did. The man quickly shouted out, "I think we should do this every Saturday." They prayed together, just the two of them, for eight months, and God began to do miraculous things in the church. Not only was the brother's marriage restored, but people began to come to the church, and many were saved. God spoke to Evans' heart and said, "If you want church growth, you have to build a powerful prayer base. This is the foundation of church growth." The church may have many activities, but it will not grow unless it is under-girded with a strong prayer base. God told Evans to invite other members of the congregation to join them for weekly prayer for the church. God blessed their commitment. The church grew from 150 members to 3,500 attending and 1,600 involved in home cells. Three hundred people committed to give one day a week to pray and fast for the church and for the pastor (Evans 1-4). God showed Evans through his failures that the only way to build God's house is through direct communication with God. "Unless the Lord builds the house, its builders labor in vain" (Ps. 127:1). Evans and the congregation learned that the vision for ministry must come from God, and the key to church growth is prayer.

Church leaders and laity alike must recognize the importance of humbling ourselves to God and acknowledging total dependence on God. God wants to bless us, but we must yield ourselves to the ways of God. His ways are higher than our ways, and His thoughts are higher than our thoughts. God knows what He is doing and why. We are called to have faith in God and to trust Him, not to try to usurp His authority. The song that is often sung for the invitation to Christian discipleship at the conclusion of the sermon is "I Surrender All." How many people have really surrendered all to Jesus? If the church would sincerely surrender all to the Father, through prayer and living out the faith, there would be love, peace and unity in the Body of Christ. The challenge for leaders and all believers is to humble ourselves so that God can lift us up. He is not a respecter of persons; He loves all of us the same. All God asks is that we spend quality time with Him daily in prayer and personal devotion. It is during those quiet times that

God reveals His plan for each life and his vision and purpose for each church.

David loved God so much that he was in constant communication with Him. He said that even on his bed, his thoughts turned to God throughout the watches of the night (Ps. 63:6-8); and early in the morning he longed to be in the presence of the Lord: *"Awake, harp and lyre! I will awaken the dawn. I will praise you, O Lord, among the nations; I will sing of you among the people."* Prayer must be the main business of the church.

Dr. Kingsley A. Fletcher contends that some prominent churches have stopped seeking the Lord through prayer and fasting. The result, he said, is that they started an immediate spiritual decline but did not realize it. He reflected on a church that at one time moved in the supernatural. Miracles, healings, signs and wonders accompanied the preaching and teaching of God's Word. Now, Fletcher said, they had to rely on gimmicks to keep the crowd coming. According to Fletcher, this decline is due to the "name it and claim it movement" in which the people put an emphasis on "faith" talk without seeking the God of faith. "Faith depends upon a strong relationship to God. A strong relationship to God can be built by 'seeking Him.' And prayer and fasting is [*sic*] the best ways to seek Him" (Fletcher 30).

We should never be too busy to pray. When we allow the demands of schedules to interfere with our prayer time, we forfeit the blessing of fellowship with our Lord and hearing His divine directions for the day. Martin Luther, father of the Protestant

Reformation, was always busy, yet he did not allow his workload to diminish the importance of spending quality time with God. In fact, he prayed for three hours daily, and God honored him with revelation knowledge and insight into His holy Word.

Rev. Dr. Cecelia Williams Bryant speaks of the divine revelation that is received in praying "The Lord's Prayer:"

Prayer, as the Mother Discipline gives birth to my spiritual life, nourishes, guides and instructs me. The praying of the Lord's Prayer ignites the mystery of the Resurrection in my spirit and I am drawn into a profound consideration of the magnitude of Christian faith. Quite simply: "He is RISEN," certainly worthy of a 24-hour feast of the Spirit. The praying of the Lord's Prayer ushers me into an absolute awareness of the redeeming Love of God for Creation in its totality and for those whose sorrow is particularly African (Bryant 81).

Dr. Preston Washington argues that prayer is fundamental to church renewal:

Prayer is the key to church renewal. . . those engaged in pastoral ministry certainly must cultivate a disciplined prayer life. But so must those in the pew. Too many church prayer meetings are helter-skelter events without intenationality or design. The goal of prayer is empowerment – to "call down" the kingdom of God into the lives of lay members and ministers and into the congregation's collective life. Communal prayer helps us to overcome our self-centeredness and begin to focus attention on the needs of the other persons in the group, their family concerns, and issues that affect the neighborhood or the community at large (Washington 4).

God will come to the aid of His people when we humble ourselves, call out to Him in prayer, stop the infighting, stop the competition, and remember that the mission of the church is to glorify God and fulfill the Great Commission. This cannot be done based on human strength or human intellect alone. God has graciously made His power available to the church through the third person of the Trinity, God the Holy Spirit, who will bring renewal to the church if we pray continually, and live holy:

> The holiness we are seeking is not a legislative or legalistic set of rules; it is Christ's very own quality of life. The Holy Spirit works in us not merely a new desire to love, but He imparts to us Christ's very own love. We develop more than just a general faith in Jesus; we actually begin believing "like" Jesus, with "His" quality of faith. It is "God in us" that makes us holy (Frangipane 115).

God is not looking for extraordinary people to bring renewal; He is looking for people who have a pure heart and clean hands, those who have a burning desire to effect change for the glory of God. Throughout church history, the Holy Spirit has empowered ordinary people to lead renewal. From the Protestant Reformation of the sixteenth century to the Pentecostal and Charismatic renewal movement in the twentieth century, those who have made a difference and ushered in reform have been believers who have refused to compromise the Gospel of Jesus Christ.

God has given the church the responsibility to lead the world based on the honorable model of leadership of the Lord Jesus Christ. If the church will follow Jesus' example, the downward spiral will be reversed, and the church will not die, but live! The church will experience spiritual growth and numerical growth, as it did in the first century (Acts 2:41, 47).

Renewal of the church will come through prayer for the baptism in the Holy Spirit and the use of spiritual gifts. Prayer places believers in a spiritual realm whereby we can receive Jesus' gifts of the baptism in the Holy Spirit (Acts 1:4, 8; 2:1-4). Why are these ingredients necessary to bring renewal?

> When we are baptized in the Spirit, we receive power to witness for Christ and work effectively within the church and before the world (Acts 1:8). We receive the same divine anointing that descended on Christ (John 1:32-33) and on the disciples (Acts 2:4; see 1:5), enabling us to proclaim God's Word (Acts 1:8; 4:31) and work miracles (Acts 2:43; 3:2-8; 5:15; 6:8; 10:38). It is God's intended purpose that all

Christians experience the baptism in the Holy Spirit throughout this age (Acts 2:39).

In the area of service, the Holy Spirit gives spiritual gifts to individual members of the church to edify or strengthen the church (1 Cor. 12-14). These gifts are a manifestation of the Spirit through individuals by which Christ's presence, love, truth and righteous standards are made real to the fellowship of believers for the common good (1 Cor. 12:7-11) (Stamps 1654-55).

Seven Elements of Prayer

God impressed on my heart that there are seven elements that will help believers focus in our prayer time. I have included one of the elements in the prayer at the end of each chapter to serve as a guide. They are:

- Sincere – Your heart must be sincere (Heb. 10:22).
- Sacrifice – Offer God a sacrifice of praise (Heb. 13:15).
- Surrender – Confess all sinful ways to God (1 John 1:9).
- Sovereign – Submit your will to God's sovereign will (Matt. 26:42).
- Supplication – Present your request to God with thanksgiving (Phil. 4:6).
- Sustains – Don't give up. Wait and believe! (Heb. 10:23, 35-36).

- Solace – Feel God's comfort; receive God's empowerment (2 Cor. 1:3-5).

Action Plan:

Prayer for Church Renewal Service

Design a Prayer for Church Renewal Service. The purpose of the prayer is to encourage people to pray together, to get excited about prayer, and to expect God to empower the congregation for life, witness and ministry. Four Sundays before the Prayer for Renewal, insert blank prayer agenda cards in the bulletin and tell the congregation that you would like their involvement in writing the prayer agenda for the event. They should include all the areas that they would like the church to include in corporate prayer. Make sure the children have an opportunity to include their prayer requests. Repeat this announcement and insert the cards in the bulletin every week until the Prayer for Church Renewal Service.

In preparation for this great event, the ministers and prayer ministry will pray and fast (you set the specific time based on the needs of your congregation) and seek God's guidance for the Prayer of Renewal. Pray that the people will be baptized in the Holy Spirit and that gifts of the Holy Spirit will be manifest in the sessions They will also pray over the prayer agenda cards, categorize the prayer requests, and make a prayer agenda that will be passed out to everyone on the day of the Prayer for Renewal. Make sure it is well publicized and invite the entire congregation to attend. Assign ministers and officers of the church to call every member to encourage them to come and pray together as a church family. Make sure the musicians are there to lead the people in worship and to join in the prayers. The attire should be casual so that everyone will feel relaxed.

The pastor will appoint members of the prayer ministry to lead different sections of the workshop, but the pastor should open the Concert of Prayer and set the tone for the morning. A suggested day and time is Saturday 9:00-12:00 p.m., but select a time that is convenient for your congregation.

The prayer leader will ask the people to form groups of no more than three persons, so that each person will have an opportunity to pray through the seven elements of prayer at the appropriate time. Initially, all the people will assemble together in the general session, and the prayer leader will announce the first category for prayer (e.g., Sincerity), read the Scripture and lead the people in song. After singing, the people will be instructed to go to their assigned prayer group (remember, no more than three persons per group), and the people will pray together for seven minutes. At the end of the time, the leader will call the people back together and introduce the second element of prayer (Sacrifice), read the Scripture, lead in song, and then instruct the people to return to their assigned groups for another seven minutes of prayer. And the program will proceed until they have finished the prayer agenda. You may want to take a break half way through the agenda and give people an opportunity to share testimonies and get refreshments. The closing will be a plenary session with everyone together. The pastor will make remarks, invite people to comment on the experience and offer a closing prayer.

CONCLUSION

Spiritual renewal will come to the church if the Body of Christ will commit to:

- A life of prayer and sanctification
- Study the person and work of the Holy Spirit
- Pray for and receive the baptism in the Holy Spirit
- Walk in the fullness of the Spirit daily
- Use spiritual gifts for building up the church

As mentioned earlier (see Chapter 3), when we are renewed, we have greater love for God and for one another. We will have spiritual zeal to read and study God's Word, and our prayer life will intensify. Moreover, we will seek to live a sanctified life, to serve in the church, to evangelize for Christ, to promote social reform, and to help improve the quality of life for others. Genuine renewal always results in a closer relationship with the Lord Jesus Christ and a passion for ministry.

It is time for the Body of Christ to unite and lead the world based on the Word of God. May God be glorified as the Holy Spirit leads the church into a new era of spiritual renewal.

PRAYER

(Solace)

Most Gracious, Sacred, Holy Father,

I bow before You with praise and thanksgiving to You, the God of compassion and the God of all comfort. Thank You for comforting Your Church through the dark days in which it seemed like corruption and false teachers would destroy the Church. Thank You for rising up in defense of the Body of Christ and comforting us in all of our troubles brought on by those who compromised the Gospel of Jesus Christ. We take solace in knowing that you hear our prayers and that You have prepared a blessing <u>for those who believe in the renewal of the church through the ministry of the Holy Spirit</u>. In Jesus' name. Amen. (2 Cor. 1:3-5).

CLOSING PRAYER

Holy Father, forgive us again for our sins, and please send renewal to the church through prayer, the baptism in the Holy Spirit, and Spiritual gifts. Please create a clean heart within us so that we will live holy before you and make disciples of Jesus Christ. We will fail on our own, but we will be victorious if we follow the leading of the Holy Spirit. Thank you Abba Father for the great gift of Your Spirit.

Now to him who is able to do immeasurably more than all we ask or imagine, according to His power [The Holy Spirit] that is at work within us, to him be glory in the church and in Christ Jesus throughout all generations, for ever and ever! Amen. (Eph.3:20).

APPENDIX A

PRE-TEST QUESTIONNAIRE OF THE BAPTISM IN THE HOLY SPIRIT AND USE OF THE SPIRITUAL GIFTS

Rev. Dr. Gwendolyn Long Cudjoe

Church Affiliation_____
Service in the Church_____
Age_____ Gender_____ F_____ M_____
Marital Status_____

Have you accepted Jesus Christ as your Lord and Savior? _____Yes _____No

If you are not saved, would you like for me to pray for you? _____Yes _____No

Why are you participating in the study?

What are your personal goals? What do you want to achieve personally from this study?

What are your goals for your church? What would you like to see happen in the church as a result of this study?

What commitments are you willing to make to the successful completion of this course (e.g. read the material, ask questions, pray, meditate on the Word of God, attend all the classes, etc.)?

Do you have a personal devotional time with God daily? If so, how much time do you spend with God? How do you structure your time with God?

If you do not have a personal devotional time with God daily... why not? Do you think it is important? If not, please explain.

If you think it is important, what prevents you from having a personal devotion time?

How would you define the Holy Spirit?

Is the Holy Spirit a "person" or a thing? Please explain.

What is the ministry of the Holy Spirit?

Where is the Holy Spirit?

What does it mean to be baptized in the Holy Spirit?

How would you define the gifts of the Holy Spirit?

What are your Spiritual Gifts (as you understand them right now)?

Are you using your spiritual gifts?

Do you feel that Christians need to be renewed in the Spirit?

How will renewal help individuals personally and the church corporately?

What steps can be taken to bring about spiritual renewal?

Please share other thoughts and comments you may have.

APPENDIX B

SYLLABUS
YOUR SPIRITUAL GIFTS CAN BRING
RENEWAL TO YOUR CHURCH

Rev. Dr. Gwendolyn Long Cudjoe

Required Text:

Wagner, C. Peter. <u>Your Spiritual Gifts Can Help Your Church</u> Ventura: Regal Books, 1994

Optional Reading:

Garmon, Lindsey. <u>Identifying and Development of Your Spiritual Gifts</u> (articles). Corpus: Church of Christ, 1996

Gilbert, Larry. <u>How to Find Meaning and Fulfillment Through Understanding the Spiritual Gift Within You.</u> Lynchburg: Church Growth Institute, 1992

Spiritual Gifts Inventory. Lynchburg: Church
Growth Institute, 1992

Bibles:
Full Life Study Bible, NIV
Spirit Filled Life Bible, NKJV

Learning goals of this study:

1. To study the history of spiritual gifts.
2. To gain knowledge in identifying and using
   spiritual gifts.
3. To spark the flame of renewal within the
   Church.
4. To develop skills in teaching as a means to
   encourage the people of God to become
   excited about the Gospel and live out the faith.

Please Note:
At the first session of this weekly Bible study, each
person will be given a questionnaire on the Gifts of
The Holy Spirit. This pre-test tool will be used to
assess each person's understanding of the topic.

COURSE INTRODUCTION

I. Who is the Holy Spirit?

   A. Old Testament Witness
   B. New Testament Witness
   C. Personality of the Holy Spirit (see handout)

II. Overview of the "Work of the Holy Spirit" in relation to:

A. Creation and Revelation
B. Jesus Christ
C. The Church
D. Individual Believers
E. Sinners

III. The Gifts of the Holy Spirit

A. Rom. 12; 1 Cor. 12; Eph. 4
B. Rediscovery of Spiritual Gifts
C. Classical Pentecostal Movement
D. Charles Parham and William J. Seymour
E. Azusa Street Revival
F. Insight to Spiritual Gifts

IV. Identify Your Spiritual Gifts:

A. Spiritual Gifts Inventory by Larry Gilbert
B. Wagner-Modified Houts Questionnaire by C. Peter Wagner (pgs. 237-252).

V. Review Definitions and Characteristics of Spiritual Gifts

A. Holy Spirit Gifts and Power by Paul Walker
B. The Primary Gifts of the Holy Spirit
C. Wagner, 253-258
D. Gilbert, 75-126

VI. The Gifts are for the Body of Christ

A. Personal Renewal
B. Renewal of the church
C. Church Growth (Wagner, pgs. 215-226)

CONCLUSION:

VII. A post-test instrument will be designed to measure and evaluate:

A. Students' Understanding of Spiritual Gifts
B. Students' Understanding of Personal Renewal
C. Students' Understanding of Church Renewal

VIII. Students will complete a Course Evaluation Form

APPENDIX C

POST-TEST QUESTIONNAIRE

Rev. Dr. Gwendolyn Long Cudjoe, Teacher

Question 1.   After studying spiritual gifts, do you understand the meaning and purpose of the gifts? Please explain.

Question 2.   List three things you have learned in this study.

Question 3.   How has this study helped you spiritually?

Question 4.   What are your dominant gifts (list the three highest scores)?

Question 5.   How can the gifts be used to bring renewal to the church?

Question 6.   How can the gifts help your church
                grow?

Question 7.   Based on your spiritual gifts,
                where should you serve?

Question 8.   Where are you currently serving in
                the church?

Question 9.   What changes should you make to
                use your gifts?

APPENDIX D

COURSE EVALUATION

Rev. Dr. Gwendolyn Long Cudjoe, Teacher

Comment on the course content: Did you receive enough information to aid in your understanding of spiritual gifts?

Comment on the method of teaching: Was the material presented clearly?

Strengths (positive):

Weaknesses (negative):

I especially liked or disliked:

My overall opinion is:

Source: This form was adapted from the course evaluation form at Houston Graduate School of Theology.

Works Cited

Adams, John Hurst.*The Doctrine and Discipline of the African Methodist Episcopal Church 1996-2000*. Nashville: AMEC Sunday School Union, 1997.

American Bible Society. *Proclaiming Grace and Freedom: Two Centuries of American Methodism*. New York: American Bible Society, 1976.

Anderson, Leith. *Dying for Change.* Minneapolis: Bethany House Publishing,1990.

Anderson, Vinton Randolph. *African Methodist Episcopal Church Hymnall*Nashville: The African Methodist Episcopal Church, 1984.

Babcock, Gary D. *Light of Truth and Fire of Love: A Theology of the Holy Spirit.* Grand Rapids: William B. Eerdmans Publishing Co., 1997.

Barna, George. "Annual Study Reveals America is Spiritually Stagnant"(Internet) 2001.

_____.*User Friendly Churches.* Ventura: Regal Books, 1991.

Barr, William R., and Rena M. Yocom, Ed. *The Church in The Movement of The Spirit.* Grand Rapids: William B. Eerdmanns Publishing Co., 1994.

Bearden, Harold I. *A.M.E. Church Polity.* Nashville: The AMEC Sunday School Union, 1984.

Bennett, Dennis and Rita.*The Holy Spirit and You: A Study of The Spirit Filled Life.* Plainfield: Logos International, 1972.

Bickersteth, Edward Henry. *The Holy Spirit: His Person and Work.* Grand Rapids: Kregel Publications,1959.

Bromiley, G.W., Ed. *The International Standard Bible Encyclopedia.* Grand Rapids: William B. Eerdmanns Publishing Co., 1989.

Bryant, Cecelia Williams. *Kiamsha.* Baltimore: Akosua Visions, 1991.

Carter, Charles W. *The Wesleyan Bible Commentary.* Peabody: Hendrickson Publishers, 1986.

Cho, David Yonggi. *The Holy Spirit, My Senior Partner: Understanding The Holy Spirit and His Gifts.* Orlando: Creation House, 1989.

Davies, Richard. *Handbook For Doctor of Ministry Projects: An Approach to Structured Observation in Ministry.* Lanham: University Press of America,1984.

Dunn, James D.G. *Baptism In The Holy Spirit: A Re-examination of the New Testament Teaching on The Gifts of the Spirit in Relation to Pentecostalism Today.* London: SCM Press Ltd., 1970.

Elwell, Walter A. and Robert W. Yarbrough. *Encountering the New Testament – A Historical and Theological Survey.* Grand Rapids: Baker Books, 1998.

Encarta. "Protestantism." Microsoft Encarta Online Encyclopedia. 2001.

Erickson, Millard J. *Concise Directory of Christian Theology.* Grand Rapids: Booker Book House, 1986.

Evans, Andrew. *Church Growth through Prayer.* (Internet) Renewal Journal #2 (93:2), Brisbane, Australia, pp. 37.

Evans, Tony. *The Promise: Experiencing God's Greatest Gift, The Holy Spirit.* Chicago: Moody Press, 1996.

Felder, Cain Hope. *Stony The Road We Trod.* Minneapolis: Fortress Press, 1991.

Fortune, Don and Katie. *Discover Your God Given Gifts.* Grand Rapids: Chosen Books.1997.

Foster, J. Curtis, Jr. *The African Methodist Episcopal Church Makes Its Mark in America.* Nashville: Henry A. Belin, Jr., Publisher, 1976.

Frangipane, Frances. *Holiness, Truth and The Presence of God.* Cedar Rapids: Arrow Publications, 1996.

Garmon, Lindsey. *Identifying And Deploying Your Spiritual Gifts.* (Internet). Corpus: Church of Christ, 1996.

Gilbert, Larry. *How to Find Meaning and Fulfillment Through Understanding The Spiritual Gift Within You.* Lynchburg: Church Growth Institute, 1992.

Gregg, Howard D. *History of The A.M.E. Church.* Nashville: Henry A. Belin, Publisher, 1980.

Jones, Charles Edwin. *The Charismatic Movement: A Guide to the Study of Neo-Pentecostalism with Emphasis on Anglo-American Sources.* Metuchen: The Scarecrow Press, Inc., 1995.

_____. *A Guide to The Study of the Pentecostal Movement: Volume Two.* Metuchen: The Scarecrow Press, Inc., 1983.

MacHaffie, Barbara J. *Her Story – Women in Christian Tradition.* Philadelphia: Fortress Press, 1986.

MacRobert, Iain. *Black Roots and White Racism of Early Pentecostalism in the USA.* Basingstoke: MacMillan Press, 1988.

McKenna, David L. *Power To Follow, Grace To Lead.* Dallas: Word Publishing, 1989.

Mead, Frank S. *Handbook of Denominations in The United States.* Nashville: Abingdon Press, 1987.

Myers, William R. *Research In Ministry: A Primer for The Doctor of Ministry Program.* Chicago: Exploration Press, 1993.

Nystrom, Bradley P. and David P. Nystrom. *The History of Christianity – An Introduction.* Boston: McGraw Hill, 2004.

Rosell, Garth. *Church History II. Audiocassette, 5. S.* Hamilton: Ockenga Institute Gordon-Conwell Theological Seminary, 1982.

Sanders, Cheryl J. *Saints In Exile:The Holiness-Pentecostal Experience in African American Religion Culture.* New York: Oxford University Press, 1999.

Schaller, Lyle E. *Tattered Trust: Is There Hope for Your Denomination?* Nashville: Abingdon Press, 1996.

Saint-Clair, Geoffrey. *Who's Who in the Reformation.* (Internet). Catholic dossier, 2001.

Scott, Elizabeth. *Anabaptists: Separate by Choice, Marginal by Force.* (Internet) The Reformed Reader, 1999-2003.

Stamps, Donald C. and J. Wesley Adams, eds.*The Full Life Study Bible New International Version.* Grand Rapids: William B. Eerdmans Publishing Co., 1992.

Synan, Vinson. *The Holiness-Pentecostal Tradition – Charismatic Movements in the Twentieth Century.* Grand Rapids: William B. Eerdmans Publishing Co., 1997.

_____*The Origins of the Pentecostal Movement.* (Internet) Tulsa:Oral Roberts University, 2002.

_____*The Holiness-Pentecostal Movement in The United States.* Grand Rapids: William B. Eerdmans Publishing Co., 1971.

Turner, Henry McNeal. *Methodist Polity.* Nashville: A. Lee Henderson, Publisher, 1986.

Vaughn, Delbert P. *On Baptism and the Holy Spirit in the Writings of the Early Church Pastors.* Houston: The Enchiridion Publishing Co., 1980.

Vine, W.E., Merril F. Unger, and William White, Jr., eds. *Vine's Expository Dictionary of the Old and New Testaments in One Volume*. Nashville: Thomas Nelson Publishers, 1985.

Wagner, C. Peter. *Your Spiritual Gifts Can Help Your Church Grow*. Ventura: Regal Books,1994.

Walker, Paul. "Holy Spirit Gifts and Power." Quoted in Jack W. Hayford, ed. *The Spirit-Filled Life Bible*. Nashville: Thomas Nelson, Inc., 1991.

Washington, Preston Robert. *God's Transforming Spirit: Black Church Renewal*. Valley Forge: Judson Press, 1989.

Printed in the United States
20942LVS00001B/132

9 781594 676925